Deliverance To Destiny

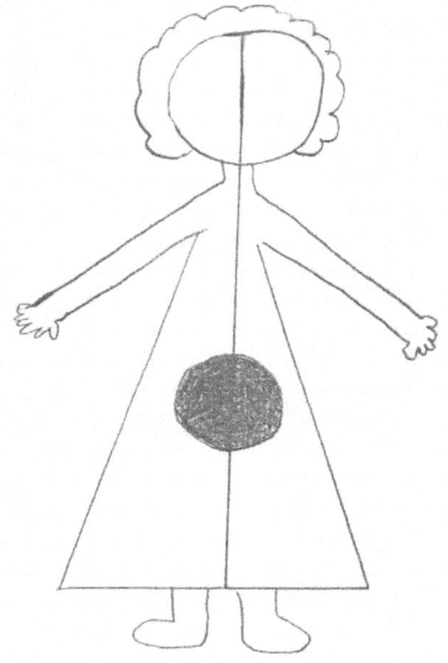

The Split Child
Out of Darkness into Light

By Sharon Ganz

No part of this publication may be reproduced, stored in a retrieval system or transmitted in any form or by any means, electronic, mechanical, photocopying, recording, scanning or otherwise, except as permitted under Section 107 or 108 of the 1976 International Copyright Act, without the prior written permission of the author.

Sharon Ganz

Sharonganz7@gmail.com

Copyright 2020 by Sharon Ganz

Distributed by Lulu Publications

I want to dedicate this book to God the Father, Jesus His Son, and the Holy Spirit who brought healing and wholeness to me through prayer. It has been a truly amazing journey. My multiple personalities and I are ONE grateful and healed heart today.

Roger, you were truly a blessing and a gift to me. The Lord hand-picked the perfect vessel I needed. Who would have believed that someone from a Baptist background would have such knowledge, expertise, and command of the demonic realm? Your gift in understanding the demonic realm facilitated and made way for my multiple personalities to surface, be healed, and become one with me. I am forever grateful.

I also want to dedicate this book to my sister Lola, who never found wholeness here on earth. She took her abuse to the grave, and she is now whole in the Savior's arms.

I also want to dedicate this book to my husband Dave who worked countless hours, rereading and correcting the pages of this book.

I am grateful for Connie my friend and scribe. She spent many, many hours supporting me through my therapy sessions taking notes. Thank you for your time and love.

For all who were a part of my Safety Net along the way--my counselors, my pastors, my doctor, and my friends who were with me for my long and difficult journey--thank you. I could have never made it without all of you.

Love,
Sharon

Contents

A week before attending a weeklong conference on PRAYER at Peniel Bible Conference I had a dream/vision (1987).

The dream was about a LOST CHILD. It was SNOWING and several people were headed into the woods looking for this lost child. I was standing to the LEFT of the scene, and in the CENTER was a MALE PRAYING. His spirit went up towards HEAVEN and I saw my spirit connect to his. His spirit was RED. (RARELY DREAM IN COLOR)

> I felt the Lord was telling me that I would find my lost inner-child through prayer. I got a sense that the search would take others on different paths as they headed into the woods and that was OK. This dream occurred shortly before the sexual abuse surfaced.

The following is my testimony and journey of the healing of my multiple personalities. The names and locations have been changed for privacy reasons.   I have been blessed by ministries, and I share their names because they were part of my healing process. My experiences with these ministries do not represent any endorsement from them.

Forward

This book is **ALL ABOUT JESUS** and is important as it delves into the darkness of Satanic Ritual Abuse and biblical brokenheartedness which the secular world calls Dissociative Identity Disorder or multiple personalities. Many events described in the following pages may be difficult to accept, even though they are happening all over our country, rather we choose to believe the reality or not.

 The author shares many shocking events that took place in her personal life as a child. My prayer is that it will serve to awake the Christian community to the evils that surround us. The Bible says much about the spiritual warfare in which we find ourselves, but all too often we choose to ignore what it says and pretend that evil doesn't exist around us. It does!

I was privileged to work with the author beginning in November of 2015 with the last counseling session completed in December 2019. During that period we all interacted together, the author, her alternate personalities and the Lord Jesus Christ, the "Wonderful Counselor." I considered myself as a facilitator as Jesus worked step by step through the counseling to bring the author to full healing and complete integration of the alter personalities. After all, one of the reasons we are told in the Bible that Jesus died on the cross was to heal the brokenhearted. This is true biblical brokenheartedness. The interactions of Jesus are well documented throughout the book. Believe it! It happened!

Jesus is the Wonderful Counselor and He was amazing in the sessions as He interacted with us, and worked with each of the alters in very simple, beautiful, tender ways in walking through the healing process. The reader will be amazed. Often He related His sufferings to the suffering experienced by the alter personalities.

As a Christian counselor I have been amazed as I witnessed how Jesus has counseled and healed through the years. It has been a privilege. Is Jesus real? Yes! Is Jesus alive and well? Yes! Will Jesus ever leave or forsake us? No! Does Jesus love us? Yes! Does the Bible say He is the

Wonderful Counselor? Yes! Then why not lean on Him and allow Him to counsel and heal.

Before the reader turns to the following pages and unfolds an unbelievable but true story of Satanic Ritual Abuse and unbelievable trauma inflicted by family members and others, a bit of basic understanding needs to be presented.

Alternate personalities are formed as a result of severe trauma (sexual, physical, or emotional) that is beyond the ability of the individual to handle emotionally. At the height of the trauma the soul (the heart of man) splits and an alter personality takes control and absorbs the worst of the trauma so that the birth person can continue to function. The birth person has no memory of the trauma due to the fact that the alter personality absorbed it. From that point on the alter personality continues to live in that memory unless and until healing occurs for the alter. Alters generally have their names and usually, not always, remain the age at which the trauma occurred. That is why in this book you will meet many young alter personalities. Healing occurs as the alter is freed from the trauma, finds peace, and then is willing to reintegrate back into the birth person's soul.

Satanic Ritual Abuse (SRA) can be defined as psychological, sexual, spiritual, and/or physical assault forced on an unwilling human victim, and committed by one or more Satanists according to a prescribed ritual. The primary aim of the rituals is to fulfill their need to worship Satan. In recent years many states have enacted laws concerning the ritual abuse of children. One law worthy of reference as the reader begins this book is the Illinois Public Act #87-1167 effective January 1, 1993 RITUALIZED ABUSE OF A CHILD.

Also you will find in the following pages the use of a conference room and conference table. This is a conference room in the author's soul in which Jesus met at times with the alter personalities. I have witnessed through the years quite often when working with SRA and other severe trauma that a conference room would be set up to help the alters feel safe as they are counseled.

The reader may question whether what happened to the author in this book is common or rare. Let me say it is not uncommon and is happening all over our country. If you know of anyone who may have been subjected to Satanic Ritual Abuse (SRA) or other severe trauma and is looking for help, have them give me a call. My prayer is that you will be informed as well as blessed at how Jesus dealt with the author and her alters in such a loving personal way through the healing process. God bless you as you move forward through the pages of this book. To Jesus be all glory!

Roger Boehm, Ph.D., cPsy
Center for Christian Counseling

Chapter One

MY LIFE AND TESTIMONY

Isaiah 49:15-16
**15 Can a mother forget the baby at her breast and have no
compassion on the child she has borne? Though she may forget, I
will not forget you!**
**16 See I have engraved you on the palms of my hands; your walls
are ever before me.**

My Childhood

My name is Sharon. I was born in a hospital not far from my
grandparent's home. I lived with my grandparents Nana and Bop until I
was six. I remember Nana as loving and kind and Bop frightening and
abusive. Bop was obese, a gambler, and an alcoholic. I remember
shaking when I was in Bop's presence. He would always say to me, "Do
you have ants in your pants?" When I was in kindergarten, I often told
the crossing guard to tell my grandfather I walked the other way home
just to avoid being alone with him in the car. I have no memory of why I
shook in front of Bop. I remember seeing a case of alcohol sitting on the
porch just off the kitchen. My grandfather would lock himself in his
room for days, drinking and howling like a madman.

I always thought my mother and Lola, my older sister by two
years, lived with me at my grandparent's house, but actually I have not
one memory of them being there. There are no pictures anywhere of me
as a baby or toddler, but there were several of my sister Lola. Somehow

my existence seemed so unimportant. What was it about this family that I was born into that they chose not to celebrate my birth?

When I was four years old, my mother had remarried, and I do remember being at their wedding. Then my mother, step-father, and Lola moved into a home thirty minutes away, but I was not to be part of the family until I completed kindergarten. I had visited my parents and Lola on the weekends, so I have been told, but I have no memory of that. I did rejoin the family when I entered first grade.

I always thought of my step-father as my dad. He is the only dad I ever knew. He was the enabler in our alcoholic family, and I remember he always told us things would get better, which they never did. My dad was lots of fun. He played softball with us, and I remember he had me reading stories to him. He had time for us and did the best he could in very difficult circumstances.

Throughout my childhood my mother struggled with obesity, alcohol, prescription drugs, and was in and out of mental institutions. I never bonded with my mother. She was never there for me. As far back as I can remember I sought my mother's love, affirmation, and approval, which never came, and I became a fighter trying to survive growing up in an alcoholic family.

My mother constantly told me things like:
- You were captured, never born
- Your father didn't want you
- You can't do anything right

What was it that drove her to say such hurtful things to me? Since my sister and I had the same biological father, why didn't my mother say those hurtful things to her as well? Eventually my mother and dad had other children, but my mother's hatred seemed to be focused on my birth, my father, and me.

One clear memory that I have as a child was the night I went into my mother's bedroom feeling afraid and needing help. When I woke my mother, she screamed and cursed, telling me to leave her alone. I remember standing in the living room that night making a vow that I would never ask for her help again. I pretty much knew I was on my own.

My Baptism and Lola's Painful Upbringing

I was thirteen years old when a neighbor took me to a Baptist Church. I remember the altar call, the tug on my heart, and the aisle I walked down that day when I went forward to accept Jesus as my Savior. I had little understanding of God, but it was clear I was a sinner and needed help. I was baptized several weeks later. My mother had punished my sister Lola that day and wouldn't allow her to go to church and witness my baptism. I was alone with no family present for what was a life-changing event for me.

My sister Lola was not only dealing with growing up in an alcoholic family, she had been sexually abused by several neighbors by the time she was ten. At around fifteen Lola attempted suicide and shortly after that her boyfriend from church shot himself. They both wound up in the hospital only a block from where I was attending high school.

Attending high school and church was painful for me. Rumors spread around the school and the church. I could not hide from all of the shame hidden within and all of the shame that surrounded my life.

Neither the school nor the church addressed my pain or offered comfort for what our family was going through with my sister's suicide attempt. It was now survival at all cost.

A Court Experience

Then came the most painful experience of my teenage years when my mother took both my sister and me to court to "get rid of us." The charge: we were both "incorrigible." Not only had my biological father abandoned me, so had my mother. Not being wanted settled deep into my being.

My dad fought to defend both Lola and me in court, and the court sought to relieve a bad situation. The court ordered my sister removed from our home. Lola moved in with an aunt and uncle for a short time before she ran away and lived on the streets of a large city, where she was eventually raped and shot. Lola eventually moved farther away, and I lost contact with her for almost fifteen years.

In the midst of all this pain, whatever had begun as God's tug on my heart in church was lost. Prayer seemed to make my life worse not better. God seemed to be distant and powerless. The hatred I felt toward my mother grew. This consuming emotion was a great obstacle to my relationship with God and His love.

I graduated high school at seventeen years old and, at my mother's request, left home. I thought it would be an opportunity to escape the alcoholic family I grew up in and finally put my life together. But denial and a geographic move would only bring temporary relief from the traumatic childhood I wanted to forget.

Marriage

I met my husband Dave while I was working for his dad. We dated for a few years, and when I was twenty-two and Dave twenty-eight, we got married in the church where I was baptized. From twenty-two to thirty life was a carefree time for me. In many ways Dave was like my dad. He was loving, gentle, patient, and kind. We eventually purchased our first home and then were blessed with two delightful girls. Jen was our firstborn and Anna followed three years later. My childhood may have been a desperate struggle, but raising our girls seemed easy. They were unbelievable gifts from God!

I called Jen "precious cargo" on our way home from the hospital. Words like strong, funny, and engaging describe Jen. At only a few months old, we put Jen on a "Crawligator," and she would maneuver her way around the entire kitchen floor - forwards, backwards, and even turning herself around. When Jen was in the crib, she would prop herself up, doing a sort of push-up, trying to get our attention when we walked past her room. Jen always wanted out of her crib. When Jen started to crawl, she never put her knees on the floor--she was up on all fours. I can still see Jen in her highchair laughing with her deep belly laugh as I played hide-and-seek with her stuffed animals.

Anna on the other hand was happy, content, and undemanding. When she was in her playpen, she just played with her toys. It was like, when you get around to it, I am here. Anna was just so easy going--just a sweet little girl.

I loved being a wife and mother. Life was so different than the chaotic childhood I had lived through. During this carefree time, I never thought about my relationship with God.

My Daughter's Illness

On a Monday evening I was asked to be a substitute in a couple's indoor tennis game. I didn't know my friend's neighbor who was my partner that night. He was a local doctor.

That weekend my two year old daughter Anna started running a very high fever, with other complications, so we took her to the hospital. The doctor I had just played tennis with on Monday was the admitting doctor that night. We recognized each other immediately. He admitted Anna. I later learned that after examining Anna the doctor suspected a mass he felt that night was a tumor.

At age thirty, my life had taken a bad turn. Anna, our youngest daughter, who was just turning two was diagnosed with Wilms tumor, a childhood kidney cancer. The next two years were hell. Surgery, a month of radiation, and eighteen months of chemotherapy brought tremendous stress and pain to our family.

The radiation treatment she needed, we were told, could damage her ovaries. Anna might never be able to have children. As of this writing, Anna is blessed with several children.

I can still see Jen at five years old standing in the kitchen saying, "I wish things were the way they used to be!" But there was no going back--difficult times lay ahead for our entire family.

Years later I would begin to understand and appreciate the depth of God's provision during Anna's illness. Six months before Anna got sick, Dave and I were vacationing in Barbados. At Sam Lord's Castle Resort, Dave and I met a vacationing couple from India who lived in a nearby state. Their daughter was the same age as our oldest daughter. When we returned home, our families spent weekends together, and we became close to both of them. My new friend just happened to be a child psychiatrist for cancer patients and her husband happened to be an oncologist! Thus, their comfort and support during Anna's battle with cancer was a gift from God. During Anna's illness we traveled with them, and I remember Anna's comment while on vacation, "No doctors here!"

Not knowing if Anna would survive, we decided to go on several vacations during her chemo treatment. If her life was going to be short, we were going to give her special times and enjoy her to the fullest.

A Gift from God

During this stressful time, our neighbor Bill came over on Christmas Eve bearing a gift. Bill had made Anna a doll house. I remember the little rooms were wallpapered, and there was even grass around the outside of the house. Special detail had gone into creating a beautiful present for Anna. Each room was equipped with furniture.

There were windows and doors, and even little people to play with. On the bottom of the house were written words of hope--that someday Anna could pass the doll house on to her daughter. Years later, that is exactly what happened!   I have realized that the Lord had come to me one Christmas Eve as a carpenter bearing a custom, handcrafted gift for my daughter to comfort us.

A Messenger from God

The following year we planned a trip to St. Croix just after Anna completed her last round of chemo. The chemo had been debilitating, but we were, hopefully, at the end of a horrible nightmare. Being in St. Croix felt like heaven. Anna's little bald head was the only reminder of what we were trying to leave behind.

We ate at a restaurant perched at the top of a hill overlooking a beautiful harbor. I was alone walking up the hill to meet my family, who had gone ahead for dinner. I stopped for a moment and sat down on a bench. My heart was filled with gratitude. I was drawn into prayer for the first time in about 15 years. In my prayer I offered thanks for the special times we had with Anna, and I offered thanks that our family was together after such a long and painful ordeal. Yet, in me was an irrational fear. Years before, I had prayed for my mother and she only got worse. I was afraid that if I prayed to God to spare Anna's life she might die.

That evening, during dinner, three entertainers sang and played their violins moving from table to table. When they came to our table, one of the men sang a song directly to Anna. The words he sang were, "Little girl, you are going to be all right."   I felt the prayer that I had prayed on the hill and the song he had sung were connected. Could he be a messenger from God? A seed had been planted. My search to seek and understand a relationship with God began.

More Provisions

Our daughter's speech and ability to talk were delayed due to her illness. Our local board of education had just started a new "Title VI – Speech and Hearing Program" for three and four year olds. My neighbor told me about it, and I inquired. They could accommodate only twenty children. Our daughter Anna got the very last opening; she was number 20! She was picked up and brought home every day by a school bus. I can still see Anna going down our hill and getting on the bus. This gave Anna something to take her mind off of her treatments. It also gave

Anna vital time to be and play with other children, and it gave me a break as well. This program was paid for by the school district, costing us nothing. This was just another way God allowed our needs to be met during my daughter's illness.

Seeking God

Living in an alcoholic family is a very painful way of growing up. I had many questions for God. If Jesus was such a loving God, why did He give so many children to my mother who didn't want them? Why did He let little children suffer with cancer, having to endure dreadful treatments to get well?

I finally wound up in a small Presbyterian Church. Pastor Joe had been there for twenty-five years. I was in my early thirties and knew nothing about Scripture, thus I knew little about God. I accepted Jesus as my Savior around age thirteen, but hardly knew what the Gospels said about Him. Pastor Joe was a very gifted teacher. On Wednesdays I would go to his two hour Bible study, not wanting to go home when it ended. I could have listened to his teaching all night long!

Around that time, God gave me an image, an image of a hand. The Lord was telling me I was the thumb. I wasn't thrilled. Sticking out like a thumb didn't seem appealing, and fitting in had been a problem for me. I didn't fit into my family of origin and fitting into church wasn't easy. I remember trying so hard to be like a woman in our church who was mild, gentle, and sweet. It was such hard work trying to be someone else. It lasted one week trying to be this finger when I was a thumb, as the Lord told me!

I took Pastor Joe's eight-week course, "What is Christianity." A barrier was blocking my view of a loving God. Study of Scripture brought me face to face with my deep hurt and anger toward my mother. My past experiences and feelings were surfacing. I felt Christ was drawing me to forgive my mother, but that seemed impossible.

After the course, "What is Christianity," Pastor Joe came to my home for a visit. I had told him that I felt Hell was right here on earth, but I had revealed nothing to him about my childhood---yet I guess he surmised much. Four hours after his visit, my sister Lola, whom I had not heard from in almost fifteen years, called. More calls came and finally her threat of suicide. The painful family past could no longer be suppressed.

I made an appointment to see Pastor Joe, and all my issues with God came pouring out. I couldn't stuff or control the pain any longer. I could hardly see God as all loving. Out it came: "I hated my mother, hated what she put us through, and hated what she did to my older sister!" The anger in me was ready to do battle with Pastor Joe, as well as God. More came out: "God was punishing me through my daughter's illness!" I was totally disarmed with the love of Jesus flowing out of my Pastor. I had waited for his condemnation and judgment, which never came. His words, "I know exactly where you are at," floored me. Pastor Joe did not tell me I had to change; he didn't tell me about the sin I was stuck in, that my hatred would destroy me. He just showed love to me. I left Pastor Joe's office that day and knew everything would be all right. I remember the drive home, with surrounding nature seeming so much brighter.

Days later I was confronted by Pastor Joe's sermon on **Philippians 2:1-2 If you have any encouragement from being united with Christ, if any comfort from his love, if any fellowship with the Spirit, if any tenderness and compassion, then make my joy complete by being like-minded, having the same love, being one in spirit and purpose.**

These words undid me. I had a need for God; Scripture came alive; and my heart was opened, though the anger in me still stood ready to do battle.

One night while I was sleeping, these words woke me, "Do not be afraid, what you read about Christ is true." I fell asleep and then woke up to the very same words for a second time, "Do not be afraid, what you read about Christ is true." I woke my husband up; then I fell asleep again; and then woke up to the same words for a third time, "Do not be afraid, what you read about Christ is true." In the morning, my husband turned to me and said, "Why did you wake me during the night?" What I knew was my experience during the night wasn't a dream. I shared my experience with Pastor Joe, and he said I had received a vision.

Shortly after this experience I was on vacation and I remember reading Luke. The Lord got my attention as I read: **Luke 1:13 But the angel said to him: "Do not be afraid," Zechariah; your prayer has been heard. Luke 1:29 But the angel said to her, "Do not be afraid," Mary, you have found favor with God. Luke 2:10 But the angel said to them, "Do not be afraid," I bring you good news of great joy that will be for all the people.** I could not help relating Scripture to the vision I had experienced, which was so similar. I had highlighted all three of these verses years ago.

Now I couldn't put my Bible down. Many days I would read from morning to night. I remember thinking now I know the Holy Spirit. I shared the vision I had experienced with a couple from our church, and they told me I was crazy. It wasn't safe to share my experiences with other Christians in this church! Near the Luke passage I wrote these words in my Bible: "So connected to God, and so alone in the church."

Moving Towards Forgiveness

Matthew 6:14 For if you forgive other people when they sin against you, your heavenly Father will also forgive you.

God immediately opened a door for me. I joined a group therapy program trying to understand the disease of alcoholism, and how it was a family disease. If I did not change my attitude, the disease would continue to hurt me and detrimentally affect my husband and daughters. As more understanding came, I began to feel sorry for my mother. I thought of how bad life had been, and realizing it was not any better for her. The truth and wisdom of Scripture was moving me beyond blame and toward forgiveness. I became convicted to surrender my mother to God, saying, "Until I can handle my feelings about my mother I dump her back on You." I also told God, "This is not a package deal involving me." There were unanswered questions – I wanted answers. It was God's problem. He was in charge and I thought He would change my mother, and I told Him I wasn't going to give Him any help loving her.

Jesus as Lord

One year later, I was reading a book called, "Lord, Why Me?" during a vacation in Sanibel Island, Florida. The Easter Sunrise sermon was titled "Eggshells and Seashells." What I was hearing was that God wanted me out of my shell. I was confronting shells on the beach all week long, and I sensed life just wasn't working like before. I found a very special place to meditate and pray. The following week I heard a sermon called, "Designed to Worship, God Speaks in Words." Which caused me to almost break down in church.

I was not prepared for what happened during that week. The book I was reading, the Easter sunrise service, and the sermon the following week revealed to me that Jesus wanted to be Lord of my life. I was frightened. How can this be? I tried to reason with God, telling

Him that I didn't have any gifts, nothing to give. I am not sure what I meant but I told God, "If you want my life, you will have to move me." At the end of the week I had surrendered with tears in my eyes at the water's edge with these words, "God, my life is yours, use me in any way you like, I'm done fighting."

That was a joke! A fighter doesn't go down that easily. I think the Lord got a chuckle out of my words.

Lola's Detox – God's Redemptive Power

My sister Lola had been detoxed in another state over 60 times. Eventually, the hospital where I attended their family therapy program took Lola into a month long detox program. The counselor told me, "Lola's chances stink in getting sober." Little did the counselor know that God's redemptive power was arranging a homecoming and a deliverance from alcohol. After a month in the hospital we took Lola into our family for a year, and she successfully made it on her own to new found sobriety. Lola spent valuable time with our family and our mother before my mother's death.

My Mother's Death - May 1983

God was slowly changing my heart regarding my mother. As I grew in knowing the heart of God, I became aware that my mother simply didn't have what I needed growing up. She was unable to give me what she didn't have herself. As I cared for my mother, I saw her as a very wounded and damaged person. I found in my heart compassion for her.

Philippians 4:19 And my God will meet all your needs according to the riches of his glory in Christ Jesus.

It was during my mother's illness that the Lord allowed our relationship to be healed. My mother was fifty-eight years old, battling both lung and liver cancer. While my mother was hospitalized, a nurse started talking to her about Heaven. I was close by and heard my mother's response, "Can you get on the train in the end?" My mother met other Christians during her hospital stay, telling me, "I met another one of your clones today!"

My mother spent the last three months of her life in my home. The hospice chaplain would come and visit my mother. One day my mother told me, "I keep falling asleep dreaming about God." I asked her, "What is God telling you?" Her comment was, "I knew I should not have told you!" My mother never shared what happened in her dreams about God, but from that moment on her life took a remarkable change. Peace was now hers. One day my mother reached up and lovingly held both her hands on my face. She thanked me for all I had done for her and told me she loved me. The love and affirmation I longed for from childhood had been expressed and now were mine.

About two weeks later, while I was telling her that I loved her, she took her last breath. A tear rolled down her face and she died in my arms. Both my mother and I had witnessed a transformation that was brought about by a loving God. What a beautiful end to not so beautiful a life. The Lord communicated to me that it was His love that would heal me.

The night they took my mother's body away, I was sitting in my bedroom, and I heard three knocks on the wall. I remember if my mother needed us she would knock on that very wall three times. I immediately went into the family room where my mother spent the last three months of her life, and with a paper and pen I wrote everything down that the Spirit of God was telling me. Inspired to do my mother's eulogy, the Lord gave me the words to share with everyone at her funeral.

Isaiah 43:1 Fear not, for I have redeemed you; I have summoned you by name, you are mine.

God can have affliction heal us and draw us near. Alcoholism took away life from my mother. The liquor hid the pain that was inside and never allowed her to heal. Alcoholism brought tremendous pain and dysfunction to the entire family. Her lung and liver cancer brought healing, allowing all of her children time to get closer when their mother was no longer in control. Though her body was wasting away she found a peace. Cancer drew my mother closer to God, and her family.

ALCOHOLISM, ABANDONMENT, AND DEATH - Fall 83
(A paper I had written)

"Sit still" seemed to be the Lord's response as I prayed for many months for direction in my life. For a compulsive person, sitting still is very difficult. I had given

up the work the Holy Spirit led me to do to devote myself to the care of my terminally ill mother. Was I meant to go back and continue the same work that I had left? My thoughts went back to my last day at Peniel Bible Conference. I had asked the group to pray for direction in my life.

Even before my mother's death, the Lord had been busy. Sister Mae, had come into my life at Easter time, and I sat through her talks on guilt, resentments, attitudes, perfectionism, and maturity. Her insight into alcoholic families was her gift from God. Jesus' love and light shone through Mae as she made herself vulnerable so others could grow. Mae had grown up in an alcoholic family, and her personal ministry in this alcoholic rehab was a moving one.

I felt the Holy Spirit had drawn me to Mae, and I sought counseling to understand the wounded child in me. Why did I have such a strong desire to delve into the suppressed pain that I carried from my childhood? Why now, just months after my mother's death?

Mae told me I needed spiritual healing for the father who brought me into this world but was never a part of my life. I have no memory of my biological father and couldn't understand why I needed healing in this area. My mother had remarried when I was very young, and I had a step-father who was a good and a loving father. I listened to Mae as she prayed for spiritual healing in my life. She also prayed that Father God would take me in His arms, hug me, and that I would feel His protection.

Days later I found myself with paper and pen writing a prayer, which led to the Holy Spirit revealing things to me. I felt peaceful as I started to write, but before long serenity left me, I felt great pain, and the tears began to flow. I began to feel grief for the relationship I never had with my biological father. He had died years ago, so there was no going back to find him. I had to accept there are parts of my past I will never know.

Since I seldom thought about my biological father, I was unaware of the feelings I had regarding abandonment. Hidden deep in me was this anger and pain. Also revealed was my anger towards God the Father.

When I wrote the prayer, my hand froze when I thought about God the Father. Some of the words in my prayer were, "I hesitate as to who and what I want to call you Lord. As I write F A T H E R, I feel confused and sad because what really is a father? I had a father who is gone—and has died. I feel the pain as I write."

As a survivor from an alcoholic childhood, I knew too well the feelings of rejection and abandonment. I now understood why I felt so different and alone, isolating me from many normal feelings and relationships. I wanted to break those painful barriers that I had built as a child to protect myself.

Christ had called me back into my childhood. The wounded child in me needed to be embraced and healed. Christ had called me to wholeness. That wholeness required a process, and spiritual healing of a wounded childhood will take time.

As the Holy Spirit guides me in the healing I know I will find the protection and trust that I did not get as a child. God the Father hugging and protecting me will be real. Mae's prayer will be more than words. As Christ's healing power works in my life, I will see many things I cannot see today.

The destructive force of alcoholism claimed the lives of both my biological parents. Their death, my wounded childhood, and the powerlessness of feeling abandoned brought forth MY NEED FOR A NEW RELATIONSHIP WITH GOD THE FATHER.

A New Church

A year after my mother's death, God opened another door for me. I moved from the church that had taught me so much about Christ's love to a large and vibrant church, which eventually offered me the opportunity to become part of their pastoral care team. Valuable training and workshops were constantly made available to those on the team.

The training prepared me to minister to hurting people. A friend and I started a 12-step recovery program that taught healing through Scripture and prayer. This outreach lasted for many years and ministered to members of eight different churches. As I studied each step while spending time in Scripture and prayer, I began to change as well. What I needed to teach was what I also needed to learn.

While at this new church the Lord stirred thoughts in me about my birth: **John 1:12 Yet to all who received him, to those who believed, in his name, he gave the right to become children of God—children born not of natural descent, nor of human decision, or husband's will, but born of God.** As I pondered the words "human decision" and "husband's will," I felt the Lord dropped the thought in me that my grandfather was my father. I tucked this insight away and never shared it with anyone.

EMPTINESS THE HOLE - October 1986
(A paper I had written)

My mother's death had opened up a floodgate of feelings in me. The emptiness caused by my childhood experiences loomed even larger. I felt raw, vulnerable, alone, and abandoned. The emptiness was an immense hole in the center of my being.

Until both my biological parents were taken from this earth, I could not fully understand or put a name to the pain that seemed to pierce my heart.

After my mother's death, I was able to reach my damaged child within, so needy, looking for affirmation, approval, and just wanting to be held, but instead was only put down and ridiculed.

There was the grief for the biological father I never knew, never lived with, and never loved. The loss of not knowing my father was not as bad as my mother's constant reminder that I was not wanted by him.

There was my sisters attempted suicide. Then there was my mother taking us to court to "get rid of us." All things suppressed as if they never existed, but the wounds were there.

The child in me fought the sadness the best way she knew how.

I thought of the death of a two-year old boy from leukemia. After his funeral, I visualized his little casket, and it was as if a part of me was in that casket too. The "little girl in me" seemed stolen—gone for good, as if swallowed up by the disease of alcoholism.

My parents had tried to fill their emptiness with alcohol. They tried to destroy their emptiness, but instead were destroyed by that very thing they used to relieve their pain. I too, tried to fill that emptiness, but instead of filling the hole with liquor I tried to fill my "hunger" (my gnawing hunger) with food, which never filled anything for long. It just made me more aware of a hole, and I am caught in the same trap my parents fell into.

The little girl in me was so needy, but this time someone heard her, someone loved her, someone was trying to touch and heal her. Jesus knew her emptiness, and He also knew what stood between the Father and His child. The Father allowed her to experience "this emptiness," to bring reconciliation of the child to her "Daddy," bringing wholeness to her in His time.

Psalm 86

I woke up on 8/25/87 in the middle of the night, and I clearly heard the words Psalm 86. Never before had I woke from sleep to be drawn to a specific Scripture. I got up to read the Psalm, and I underlined these words:

Psalm 86:1-2, 7, 11 Hear, O Lord, and answer me, for I am poor and <u>needy</u>. Guard my life, for I am <u>devoted to you</u>. You are <u>my God</u>; save your servant who trusts in you. In the day of <u>my trouble</u> I will call to you, and <u>you will answer me</u>. <u>Teach me your</u>

<u>way, O'Lord, and I will walk in your truth</u>; give me an <u>undivided heart</u>, that I may <u>fear</u> your name.

I wrote these words in the margin, "My heart is divided, and my fear is a needy child by the roadside afraid of the growling dog inside the <u>long</u> black car. My fear was not in the Lord but in my childhood." What was the Lord trying to communicate with Psalm 86 and the thoughts I had written in my Bible?

(During my childhood, I heard mention of my grandfather having a large black car).

Sexual Abuse Workshop for Clergy Fall - 1987

As part of a Pastoral Care Team I was able to sign-up to attend a sexual abuse workshop for clergy. I went with the pastoral care minister and another woman for the weekend training. I knew my sister Lola had been abused by several neighbors when she was young. I had very little memory of my own childhood and none about physical or sexual abuse; I only remembered the verbal and emotional abuse from my mother.

Two workshop pastors had taught about Satanic Ritual Abuse (SRA), sharing their knowledge and experiences. When the conference finished, one of the speakers got up and said, "I can see that someone in the front row has been triggered during the conference." That someone was me and what eventually emerged was the realization that I was a victim of bizarre sexual abuse. The Lord used this conference to break through my denial, and the fear began surfacing in me from my being victimized by a cult.

On our drive home we noticed an elderly woman walking down a deserted country road. We stopped to see if she was lost or otherwise needed help. The three of us got out of the car, and the two other women walked across the road to help her. Suddenly, a limousine pulled up and stopped, blocking me off from the others. Someone opened the back window, and a large person dressed in a dog outfit stuck his or her head out the window and growled at me. I was so frightened. The window went up, and the limousine pulled away. It was a bizarre scene for sure.

The elderly woman got into our car, and we took her back to her home, which was nearby. The other two women had no idea what had just happened to me, but they could see that something had shaken me. That started past memories surfacing of being frightened and triggered by dogs.

Depression was now my constant companion. Sleep wouldn't come, and when it did, I was plagued with disturbing dreams sexual in nature. It was Christmas time, and I remember sitting on my couch staring at the poinsettia plant in my bay window. Suicidal thoughts stirred in my head. Thoughts came of eating the poinsettia plant, or perhaps feeding it to my husband! Those thoughts frightened me. Living became a great effort, and I knew I needed help.

Pieces were coming together: the vision about a dog-man, the limousine and the dog in it, the Scripture that made me recall a dog inside a long black car, and my divided heart. Only the Lord could have helped me to pull these pieces together. I didn't know what it all meant, but clearly fear and dogs went together.

Dad's Battle with Cancer

My step-dad was diagnosed with pancreatic cancer in 1987. He lived about an hour's drive away from his grown children. His cancer diagnosis gave all of his children opportunity to spend valuable time with him on the weekends. We knew time was short.

Dad's second wife had died a few years earlier, and he had asked my youngest sister to move back with him. All of his children piled into his house on the weekends. Dad had enough room to navigate his walker around the house. He insisted we get him a horn to put on his walker just to make sure we were not in his way. He never complained. We were all left with happy times and memories. He was a special dad to the end. Dad died in his sleep on my older sister's birthday.

A Broken Leg

While teaching youth club, I fell at the church altar and broke my leg. I had not been in control. My mind falling apart, my world falling apart, and now my body was broken.

In February 1988, I flew across the country hoping a month long stay at a well-known Christian clinic in Texas would shed light on and bring answers to my pain. Now I could not cry and could not feel. These were new issues for me. I headed to the Texas clinic in a wheel chair due to my fall, having a cast on my leg and crutches at my side.

A Christian Clinic in a Hospital

I was in the clinic only a few days when the Lord gave me an image of "The Split Child."

THE SPLIT CHILD

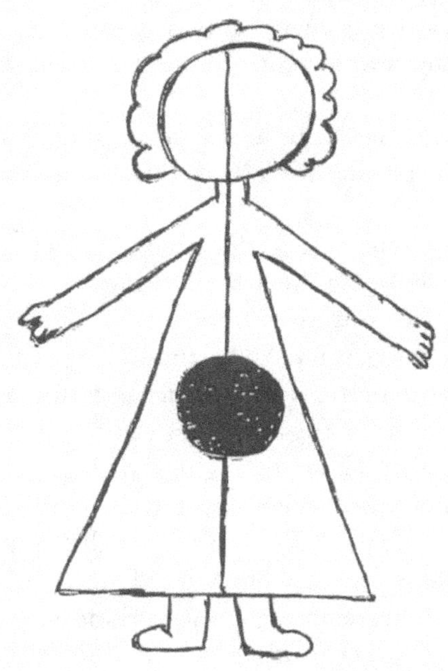

The child was completely SPLIT in half.
She had this dark HOLE in her STOMACH.

I wanted to create what I had visualized out of clay in my occupational therapy class, but they wouldn't allow me. They were ignoring what the Lord had shown me. This image was communicating something powerful regarding my childhood. I also tried to share in group therapy papers I had written but they disregarded that as well.

I also remember seeing a TV program about dogs while alone in my hospital room. I tried to bring my issue up regarding dogs in therapy, but again I was ignored.

While at the clinic, an MRI was done of my broken leg to see if I could come off my crutches. An orthopedic doctor came into my room and asked me, "What happened to you when you were small?" There had been previous trauma to my leg, and he wanted me to remember the circumstances. Standing right by my bed, the doctor could not have missed the tears that rolled down my face. I then went silent, numb and shut down. Neither the orthopedic doctor nor anyone else at the clinic asked me about my tears.

During group therapy, I was asked to read Scripture, and I went numb. What was happening to me?

While my blood was being drawn, another patient told me that I looked like I was going into a trance. Patients could see what the doctors were ignoring.

At the clinic, I was put on Prozac and started taking thyroid medicine. I was informed that I had Post Traumatic Stress Disorder PTSD.

Being at the Clinic was a negative experience. What I tried to communicate was not being heard. During my stay someone at the Clinic told my husband, during a phone call, I was "histrionic" (which meant self-centered, exaggerated, dramatic behavior that seeks attention). They dismissed the horrific pain stuffed down in me just to survive. This label did not make life easier for me when I got home.

A month at this clinic brought frustration, not answers. My counselor's last words were, "We can't help you!" I wish someone would have said, at the least, "We don't have all the answers, but Jesus is the answer." I was more broken when I left the clinic than when I arrived! I left the clinic devastated, without hope.

Years later, I met another woman a few towns away who experienced the same thing at that same Christian Clinic. Dot also had a background dealing with her multiple personalities.

Sometime after I left the clinic, I had a flashback seeing myself as a small child in my grandfather's basement sitting on his workbench with my leg in a black vise. I saw two men in front of me. The flashback ended. (Is this how my leg was broken as a small child?)

I also remember being told that I had polio when I was a child — but that turned out to be a lie and cover-up. They wanted to intimidate me and keep me from talking about what had been done to me, and by whom. I lived in constant fear: what else were they planning to do to me? Before my sister died, she said to me, "Do you remember when they told you that you had polio?" Lola knew it was a lie and so did I. (Thanks to the Lord that my sister confirmed this lie before her death).

My Issue with Doctors and a Christian Psychologist Dr. Russ

I took a substitute position as an administrative assistant in a psychology department of a Catholic University. I never addressed the doctors or staff by their titled names the entire time I was there. Before the abuse started to surface doctors were never an issue for me. I knew I was acting very strange, not addressing staff with their titles, and this was painful for me. I never shared this with anyone for fear they would not understand, thinking I was crazy.

When I returned home from the Clinic in Texas, I found a Christian psychologist. For the first six months of therapy, I wouldn't address him by any name. Then God started confronting and convicting me to talk to my therapist about why I didn't want to address him by any name or by his title—Doctor. Why was something that simple such a stumbling block? I didn't know it at the time, but doctors were part of my abuse, and that was why I could not call him by his title. When I shared with him that I needed to call him by his first name, he wasn't happy and didn't understand.

Doctors and police had been involved in my abuse. People I would ordinarily trust became a trigger for me.

I remember the psychologist quoting **Philippians 4:8, Finally brothers, whatever is true, whatever is noble, whatever is right, whatever is pure, whatever is lovely, whatever is admirable—if anything is excellent or praiseworthy—think about such things.** This Christian psychologist was ignoring my real issues and pain.

The session below will describe what the Lord put on my heart to do. The following week Russ was unable to even discuss why I acted out the way I did. He didn't go near my pain; the only thing he wanted to do was to put me on more medicine. That would be my last session with him.

Download

The Lord was speaking to me in images, dreams, and visions to expose and deal with my childhood trauma. This time the Holy Spirit gave me a "download" with clear direction. I was obedient where the Spirit was leading me.

My grandparents had always called me Sherry. I will use Sherry throughout this book. Sherry represents my inner child who endured great abuse. My parents or siblings never called me Sherry.

AGAINST ALL ODDS – 6/9/90
(A paper I had written)

I had been drawn to Michael Talbot's song, "The Hiding Place." God spoke to me as I listened to his singing of **Psalm 32:7 You SURROUND my soul with cries of deliverance. Psalm 32:10 The Lord's unfailing love SURROUNDS the man who trusts in Him,** *proclaimed God's promise to me.*

As I played this song many times, I focused on a LIE that I carried. The Holy Spirit was giving me direction regarding something that had appeared in many of my dreams: the CIRCLE. I knew I needed to claim the truth that the Lord's love surrounded me. I needed to break the LIE, break the satanic CIRCLE.

(Session at Dr. Russ's office) *What actions I am about to describe is something I would not have chosen to do on my own. It was too crazy, but I just obeyed where the Spirit was leading me.*

Prayer led me to go to a store on the highway where I searched for an hour before finding all the items I needed. My purchase comprised of a square foot piece of wood, a bamboo circle, and a camping axe. My next stop was the florist where I purchased a vase and two roses. I was to purchase a BABY ROSE and a long stem rose. I found the remaining items in my home, which included a pair of scissors, a hammer, U-shaped nails, a book on satanic abuse, and my Bible.

I headed off to my therapy session with all these items in a shopping bag. I remember my therapist Russ commenting about the look I had on my face. I was just determined to finish what I was directed to do.

I sat on the floor and took out the things I needed first. I gave Russ the book on satanic abuse, and I told him he would have to read about the CIRCLE when it was time. I lay my Bible open to PSALM 32. I took out the two roses and the vase. I cut the long-stem rose and put it in the vase. I noted that I was to take the rose home when I was done, and it was to be a reminder that I was COMPLETE and WHOLE IN CHRIST, in spite of what was in my head or how I felt.

I then asked my therapist to read about the satanic circle, and then I read PSALM 32. I claimed God's promise that the Lord SURROUNDS me. I then took the wood and nailed the bamboo circle to it. Next, I took the BABY ROSE and placed it in the center of the CIRCLE. Using the U-shaped nails, I nailed the baby rose to the wood. The BABY ROSE represented me, when I was a small child. The nails were holding me in place; they were a reminder that I was BOUND. Then I took the axe out of the bag and I proceeded to chop the BABY ROSE BUD from the stem. Then I axed the stem because my abusers left nothing. Whatever beauty I possessed had been stripped away. The baby rose bud and the stem were destroyed.

Now, I was ready to deal with the LIE of the satanic circle and destroy it. I chopped the bamboo circle in several places before my therapist raised his voice for me to STOP. Russ told me to put everything away, and we would talk about it. Obediently, I put all the shattered pieces of Sherry away, hiding Sherry once again. Her anguish lay HIDDEN away in the shopping bag.

Years later, I understood more what happened during that session. My task was that I needed to BREAK the satanic circle, but I was trying to DESTROY the CIRCLE, wanting revenge for what was done to me. Oh, how I identified with Moses disobeying God. I allowed my anger to lead me beyond what the Lord had intended.

Healing Conference 1991

We were asked to stand for prayer when we felt a need. I stood for:

- The breaking of vows. (I wanted to break the vow to never go for help)
- The breaking of generational ties
- The breaking of documents:
    Particularly the Christian Clinic—paperwork including my birth certificate, and other documents

I went forward for prayer and laid flat on the floor in front of the prayer team. They asked me what I needed to surrender. I could not believe the words; horrific detail came out of my mouth. Then I went numb. Where were these thoughts coming from? These thoughts also including "death threats" that were spoken over me as a small child. The words coming out of my mouth were confirmed, many years later. They will be verbalized by my multiple personalities later in this book. The leader of the conference put her hand on my heart and prayed that God would create a new heart within me.

OUT OF DARKNESS INTO LIGHT - 1/1/92
(A paper I had written)

I lived in despair for three years as the Lord led me through the dark night of my soul. Out of nowhere came spiritual and emotional anguish accompanied by physical reactions that tormented me. There seemed little hope for healing as the dreams, flashbacks, choking, vomiting, and bleeding sapped me of my energy, and at times, my desire to live.

It was my journey into Hell, making me wonder if I would eventually crackup or go crazy. But there seemed no way out, only through, and I thought there would be no end.

For almost forty years, horrific childhood abuse had stayed suppressed in me. As the abuse and its bizarre nature began to surface, it seemed to have a mind of its own. There were times the trauma would surface and then vanish as quickly as it appeared, leaving me confused, with doubts and fears of never being well again. How could one heal from what one couldn't even understand or explain? Sometimes my anguish felt it would burst out of me.

Surprisingly, the presence of this Enemy was most vivid for me in church. Church was no longer a refuge. Entering the church doors was like walking into a battlefield, wondering where the attack would come from next. But not choosing to go to church meant defeat. Giving up worship meant giving up my only means of survival, Christ Himself.

The darkest part of this journey occurred during the early part of 1991. Prayers about "life" and "hope" got me in touch with the depths of my pain. One day in church I wanted to shout, "I have Christ and I feel hopeless, I know Christ and I feel lifeless." Death would have been welcomed. I had little desire to continue with the life that God had given me.

The still, small voice that I had grown to know during my walk with Christ seemed inaudible. Caring for and following God's purpose had little meaning. The abuse had robbed me of a normal childhood, and there was nothing stopping it from devouring my adult life. I identified with Jesus' words, **My God, my God, why has thou forsaken me?** *And* **Father, take this cup from me.** *I knew Jesus knew my pain – His words spoke to my pierced and shattered heart.*

What got me through were several chosen vessels of the Lord. They were people found throughout my three-year journey, always crossing my path at the right time. Each person brought something different; each had a special gift God provided to me.

In the spring of 1991 at a healing conference, I met a gentle and humble servant of the Lord. Little did I know she would be performing a kind of open heart surgery on me. During the Deliverance, my heart was changed and what I doubted happened – the darkness lifted.

Tornados 1997

My pastor had been teaching about spiritual warfare when I drew on a page of Jeremiah a green Christmas tree, a small girl with a corklike screw going up though her, as well as a corkscrew next to the girl, writing these words, "corkscrew, hard, and tight." 12/11/97.

Jeremiah 17:1,2
Judah's sin is engraved with an iron tool, inscribed with a flint point, on the tablets of their hearts and on the horns of their altars.

Even <u>their children remember their altars</u> and Asherah poles beside the spreading tree and on the <u>high hills</u>.

Charismatic Christian Social Worker - Ben

Through a contact in my church I got in touch with a local counselor named Ben. He became my counselor on and off for many years as my childhood abuse began surfacing. Ben heard in his Spirit what was not heard during the month I spent at the Christian clinic.

During my therapy Ben and I were discussing Jeremiah 17, and I said, "The corkscrew looks more like a tornado than a corkscrew." When I returned home, within an hour, I had looked up Satanic Ritual Abuse and printed out an article which stated, "If they draw tornados, talk about tornados, see tornados in the system, you know for sure they've got a spin program."[1] I wasn't sure, what a Spin Program was but I knew it wasn't by accident that I drew tornados, then read about tornados.

Later, I learned the Spin Program serves to disorient the victim. I do, remember going through dizzy spells especially before my therapy sessions. Sometimes it felt like I was being tossed around in a clothes dryer.

---

[1] Mary Jo Schneller, 1999 Conference Presentation

One day Ben asked me, "If the Lord could give you one thing, what would that be?" Immediately I responded: "I wanted to see someone who made it through to the other side, who was whole and complete in Christ."

What I really liked about Ben was that at the end of each session he would save some time to go over what he felt he was hearing. This comforted me that I knew I was being heard and heard correctly.

A Pastor Understands SRA

When I was part of a pastoral care team, I was able to attend a weekend event titled Sexual Abuse Workshop for Clergy. I found out that Pastor Steve, who taught and shared his testimony at the workshop, was doing his Internship at a local church. He was abused by both his parents who were professionals yet were members of a cult. Steve was a young pastor who was a victim of what is called Satanic Ritual Abuse (SRA).

I started attending this church and its outreach to those who were sexually abused. I was looking for answers.

Over the months, I was able to share with Pastor Steve my troubling dreams and flashbacks. He was interested in the tombstone I had drawn, which had occurred in my dream. He asked me where my abuse had taken place. I told him it was nearby, and he asked me if I would be willing to go back there with him.

We prayed before we headed out. During prayer I had an image of the graveyard with something black in the center.

As we were driving through the town, just before my grandparent's home, Pastor Steve spotted a Masonic road sign. He told me that this particular organization was a cult. I told him that my grandfather was a 33 degree mason. Pastor Steve said that sometimes abusers had children's fingers cut off to mark them. Immediately, I thought of how my cousin, who was two years older than I, had several fingers missing. I told Pastor Steve this. We were all told that my cousin was born that way.

In the cemetery beside my grandfather's house, we found the exact tombstone that I had drawn. As we went up the cemetery's hill, at the center of the graveyard we spotted a black altar for a pastor and his child. I clearly heard in my head, "There it is!"

Pieces of my missing puzzle were: the road sign about Masons, my grandfather being a 33 degree mason, my cousin's missing fingers, a black altar in the center of the graveyard, and the words in my head as we approached this altar, "There it is!"

I was a Christian grounded in the Lord and yet felt unfixable—with cult-caused trauma not talked about in churches. I didn't feel safe in my church, in my own home, in my own head, and in my own body. My heart was shattered and fragmented. The abuse ended when my grandfather died. I was ten years old.

My abusers sought total power and control, violating my body, mind, and spirit. Everything I trusted, they tried to corrupt. What I held so precious: my relationship with Christ, Scripture and prayer came under attack. They twisted Scripture to degrade me, perverting it with sexual overtones. Who do you tell that to? Who will understand the struggle I had with Scripture?

The graveyard was next to my grandparent's home. The Masonic Temple was across the street, and the funeral parlor was two doors away. I had clear memory of my grandfather's black robe and a cane that hung in his closet, which were used when my grandfather individually abused me, as well as the abuse that took place during cult ceremonies and rituals. I remember fearing my grandfather.

The Lord gave me these Scriptures which promised me that He knew what had happened to me and that He would judge all who were involved in my abuse:

Matthew 10:26 So do not be afraid of them. There is nothing concealed that will not be disclosed, or hidden that will not be made known.

Hebrews 4:13 Nothing in all creation is hidden from God's sight. Everything is uncovered and laid bare before the eyes of him to who we must give account.

Flashbacks and How Memories Came

My memories came in visions, images, or dreams, which seemed disconnected, pieces in a puzzle, like seeing unconnected dots.

When you go through Satanic programming, it is against Jesus. Jesus will be introduced and used in rituals only to get you to believe untruths about him. Jesus has the power to undo evil, and Satan's followers know He is the threat. To cause confusion they will introduce someone dressed up to be Jesus. They try to make this Jesus appear weak, unable to stop what they are doing.

To program their victims at their ceremonies and rituals, they often read Scripture, instilling a negative reaction in the victim to Scripture and God. This made being in church very difficult. My mind would go numb because I could not handle the cross messages I got from Scripture and what they programed into me.

Letter to Jesus by Sharon (adult) and Sherry, her (inner child) 10/11/98
Sherry accepts Jesus as Lord

Dear Jesus,

I felt so much hurt and sorrow as I drove to church, but it was not a safe haven today, and I had to flee.

On the ride home, I listened to a song on the radio about sadness, a rose, and carrying the weight of the world. The more I listened to the song, the more it related to Sherry, my inner child. I addressed Jesus, "I am so very afraid. Who can hear my pain? Who will believe me? The people who hurt and abused me told me "I wouldn't be believed, and people would think I was crazy."

Images of being bound had been in my head for days. Today my thoughts are, "Jesus isn't the sacrifice here, you are! Jesus, I know you are truth and light. Why do I have these thoughts in my head? Is Sherry a liar? Is she making all this up? Jesus, you died on the Cross to set us free. Sherry was bound as a little girl—she could not move or get away. Jesus you rose from the grave. You have victory over death and the grave. It was a grave next to my grandfather's house you clearly led me to that shed some light on my past."
Love, Sharon

Lord,

This is Sherry speaking. Sharon surrendered me to you years ago. I know Who you are – You are God. You created the world where good and evil exists. Well, evil has touched my life as a little girl.

So my Enemy will be aware to Whom I belong: "I Sherry, accept you, Jesus, as my Lord and Savior! I belong to You and You alone! I do not know where you were when I was a little girl or why you let them destroy me. I felt like a nothing. I don't know how you heal nothing. How would you heal my body?

Your Word tells me that before the world existed it was formless and empty. Well, a little girl would describe that as being a nothing. The world before was like the way I felt, and yet by Your Authority and Your Word, you created the world from nothing.

Jesus, I belong to You. Please heal and restore the destroyed little girl. Jesus, lead me to safe people who will understand and believe me. If it isn't going to be safe, don't let them near me. Please guide and protect me.

Jesus, help me with: being bound, the grave, the rose, the devastation, feeling like a nothing, and the thought that Jesus isn't the sacrifice but I am, and baptism.

Jesus, this is beyond a little girl's understanding. HELP ME!
Love, Sherry

My Family Doctor – Dr. Jim

One day I went to my family doctor, Dr. Jim, and learned that he knew about Satanic Ritual Abuse. I was so depressed when I went to see him, and his comment to me was, "Isn't your God big enough?" Dr. Jim prayed for me before I left his office. He also told me he was going to pray and fast for me. Dr. Jim tried calling several people in the area to counsel me but found no one. He even called the very psychologist who was no help to me, with whom I had such a bad experience months earlier. It's a small world.

Counselor - Jill

The Lord allowed me to meet Jill, a pastor's wife, at a healing workshop. Jill was a licensed counselor who had knowledge of the abuse I went through. Once a month for an entire year, with a friend I drove north for an hour and half each way to get counseling. Jill counseled me for almost three hours each visit, and she would even feed us before sending us home. Jill took no compensation for our time together. Jill was a gift from God and by His grace, I recognized God's provision of her to me.

My Forum Message by Sherry 8/14/01
(An experience I had written about)

Last night, I was overwhelmed with frustration and rage. The cursing wouldn't stop in my head. I was angry for what the clinic doctors and the psychologist couldn't or wouldn't hear, for the pain they ignored and made me bury. I was at the gym for only a half-hour, but I needed to leave and process these unstoppable thoughts. I wanted to see Sara. Would she still be up? I knew Sara would understand.

Only the Holy Spirit could have brought the revelations that day. I started putting the pieces together when I was at the gym. A praise song that I had been listening to intensified my distress. I began to recall what I experienced during that day. I often play praise music in my car, and for whatever reason, I turned on the radio. Driving to work that morning, I heard a Christian psychologist on the radio (the very one who didn't hear me) talking to one of the doctors at the Christian Clinic in Texas (also, the very ones who didn't hear me) about suffering and about Job. Initially, I wasn't upset by their conversation.

At lunch, I went for a cup of coffee and returned to listening to the radio, and the Christian Clinic was on again. I was astounded at a woman who called in. Two of her daughters had accused her father (their grandfather) of Satanic Ritual Abuse (SRA). Both the girls told their mother that rats and coffins were part of their abuse. The mother defended the grandfather as a kind man. In answer to the doctors she said that she never saw her daughters dissociate into multiple personalities. As far as she was concerned, they acted normal.

I couldn't believe my ears; I was hearing mostly agreement with the mother from the doctors representing the clinic. They showed lack of understanding of DID/SRA, Dissociated Identity Disorder and Satanic Ritual Abuse. Their denial of DID/SRA had hardly changed since I was a patient at the Clinic thirteen years ago.

Also, the mother's comments about the daughter's choice of a therapist were unkind and cutting. Both the woman and the doctors were poking fun, laughing at the daughter's expense. I wonder how many other traumatized people they have damaged that came through their doors for help?

The Clinic had never responded to the image I drew while I was hospitalized -- "The Split Child." They didn't even take the time to discuss it or ask why I drew it.

Similarly, the Christian psychologist never once asked me a question about why I chose to break a circle and destroy a baby rose with a camping axe in his office. He never questioned why I brought in a satanic book and how that related to my reading of Psalm 32:10. No, all he could do was tell me to put everything away. He never referred to the session again; he only wanted to put me back on more medicine.

Dogs Were Clearly a Trigger

I was never afraid of dogs growing up, and my family had several dogs.
However, vague memories came to me of being in a crib in my grandparent's home and being frightened by a large dog. Did this relate to another repressed experience of a man dressed up as a dog?

During the period that my daughter Anna was sick, our older daughter Jen kept asking us for a dog. Since Jen was so responsible, and we knew she would take care of a dog, we found her a little puppy. It was a cross between a miniature collie and a German shepherd. "Ruffles" would let the kids do anything with him. I remember them putting him in a baby stroller with a bonnet on his head. Ruffles would love to jump into huge piles of leaves that we raked in the autumn. He was such a good-natured dog. One night while I was saying prayers with the kids, Ruffles knocked the cookie sheet off the table and ate every one of the ginger snaps before I got downstairs. After that, when I was baking ginger snaps, he would sit patiently right by the oven, waiting for the cookies to come out. Ruffles was a good dog.

For most of Ruffle's life I didn't act this way, and I never harmed him in any way, but he was aware that I didn't want to be near him. One day the pastoral care minister of my church was visiting. She loved animals and commented to me, "Your dog is afraid of you!" I felt such shame.

When our dog had to be put down, I had to make amends. How many people have to make amends to a dog? I told Ruffles that I was so sorry for the way I treated him. I told him he didn't do anything wrong, but when I was little something very bad happened to me regarding dogs.

Forgiveness

The Lord eventually helped me to forgive all the people who could not hear or understand the abuse I endured as a child. Some were Christian professionals who had no idea about this abuse. They were like my mother. My mother didn't have what I needed and couldn't give me what she didn't have, and neither could they. But I am truly grateful for all the counselors, pastors, my family doctor, and Christian friends who encouraged me and were part of my safety net on my long journey to recovery. Forgiveness opened many doors and Scripture is clear, God is the one who enables our needs to be met. **Philippians 4:19 And my God will meet all your needs according to his glorious riches in Christ Jesus.**

Abuse & Terror

Sharon and Sherry had accepted Jesus as their Savior and Lord, but my heart was hardly healed. I possessed "alters" that were overwhelmed with evil, shame and self-hate.

I remember being in my bed one night facing the window. I was wide awake, but "frozen in terror," unable to move for what seemed hours -- one of the worst nights I ever lived through.

On 7/28/01, during prayer with a friend, I saw an image of four paper dolls all in a row. My friend prayed about the fact that they were all faceless. Later I was taking a shower and the image of the paper dolls returned as they were originally. I saw this finger rub off their faces. I thought, "What is this all about?" Then the thought came to me: NO MOUTH CAN TELL, NO EYES DID SEE, NO NOSE CAN SMELL, NO EARS TO HEAR THE TRUTH.

My shower became an unsafe place. The droplets of water would start to form images on the sliding glass door. I became anxious and afraid. What image would form? For months I felt anxiety every time I took a shower.

While in prayer with Sara I saw an image of **PAPER DOLLS** all in a row. Sara prayed about the fact that they were all **FACELESS**.

I was taking a shower and the image of the paper dolls returned. I saw this finger rub off their faces. I thought, "What was this all about?" Then the thoughts came.

NO MOUTH CAN TELL
NO EYES DID SEE
NO NOSE CAN SMELL
NO EARS TO HEAR THE TRUTH

My Locket of Hope

The Lord led me to **PSALM 107:20 He sent forth his Word and healed THEM, he rescued them from the grave.**

With this Scripture, the Lord inspired me to seek a locket. I found a locket with a heart inside a heart engraved on the front. It represented the Lord being in my heart. I printed out the Scripture verse, found a picture of me at about age four and put both inside my locket. I wore the locket everywhere.

A Difficult Surrender 2002

When the most horrific part of the abuse started to surface, my counselor Ben told me, "What we have been waiting for is now happening, but I am unable to walk down this part of the journey with you." I was angry and devastated. I didn't want to go down the road without Ben.

Ben said he didn't have enough time in his schedule to give me two hour sessions, which is what he felt I needed.   He also felt the Lord was not leading him to take me any further in my healing. I trusted Ben. Why was the Lord taking him away? He did tell me he would be there for me until I found the counselor to whom the Lord would lead me.

Changing counselors was so scary. How would the Lord guide and confirm the choice?

I started attending a church close to home. I probably wrote my pastor more times in two years than I wrote to all my previous pastors combined. At times it was agonizing to hit the send button letting go of my painful thoughts. I waited for his rejection which never came. His sermons had been pushing my buttons. This pastor responded within hours to all my e-mails. He always had encouraging words. He was a blessing when things in my life were very unstable.

We were studying Moses' life in church. We were at the end of his life, studying the last chapter of Deuteronomy. My pastor was talking about how a carpenter uses specific tools in constructing a door. Each tool that the carpenter chose has its own purpose. You couldn't shave the bottom of the door with a screwdriver, and you couldn't put screws in with a chisel. The understanding I drew from his sermon was the new counselor would be a new tool the Lord wanted to use.

The Lord had used Moses powerfully in the last 40 years of his life. The Lord, chose to have Moses climb one more mountain, Mt. Nebo, because he had something He wanted Moses to see. The pastor was talking about "passing the baton" relating it to **Deuteronomy 34:9 Now Joshua!** Scripture had suggested that the Lord was passing the baton from Moses to Joshua.

Moses and Joshua were both Godly men, both with a divinely inspired purpose. Their paths were provided by God. He guided the baton being passed forward in Moses life as well as mine. God's timing was perfect. I needed to let go of my counselor Ben who walked with me for many years, because the Lord was opening a new door.

Pastor/D. Min 2002-2003

The very next day, while in prayer at the altar of my church, a woman in the church handed me a card of a counselor who was an hour's drive from my home.

I had been gifted a new wonderful Christian counselor in my life. Dr. Jack had been a pastor for 34 years when his wife was diagnosed with cancer. He left the pastorate to start an outreach for cancer victims and their families. Cancer did eventually claim his wife's life. Would this be someone who would understand the abuse and loss I had endured?

I gave Jack some images about the bizarre abuse that were surfacing in me. Jack asked me, "Would you first tell me exactly how you got my name?" He too, was trying to find out if this counselor/patient relationship was God ordained.

It was soon apparent that my emptiness from my devastated childhood was not a problem to him; he was dealing with all stages of grief and death with his cancer patients and their families on a regular basis.

Our sessions were twice a month and two hours long. I would first share what I experienced during the week. Then I would sit and listen as Jack taught me Scripture. Time in prayer followed.

I remember Jack one day saying during our prayer time, "Lord, I don't have any clue!" I remember replying, "Jack, You have to have a clue." Was I wishing my counselor to have knowledge what only God could understand? Was I still trusting human understanding over trusting The Healer? Jesus wanted me, above all, to seek Him. He (and not man) was the ultimate solution. Healing came not in finding answers, but in finding more of Jesus.

Jack said he was getting ready for work when the Lord gave him an image regarding me. He said he rarely experienced images/visions. He saw a small child lying dead, and Jesus had her by the hand and was helping her up. For weeks I had been praying about Jairus' daughter.

She had been dead, and the Lord brought her back to life. I had never told my counselor I was praying about Jairus' daughter. What I had been praying about for weeks, the Lord had given Jack an image of that very thing! Awesome!

I was in counseling with Jack for a little over a year, and our sessions ended in an unusual way. I needed to have a hysterectomy, and I also felt the Lord needed me to move on. I had real peace about concluding therapy. Another layer of the onion had been peeled and healed.

Understanding the Split between Sharon and the Alters 12/02

Before I ended my sessions with Dr. Jack, he asked would I mind if his pastor friend Frank joined us for a session. I was open to any way help would come. Afterward, I wrote to the both of them to try to put into words what I experienced.

Initially, there were two sides of me in this split. When I am in the one side the other one FADES. I have this LOGIC/BELIEVING side of me who is Sharon, a believer grounded in Christ. Then there is the FEELING side of me which represents the repressed dark pieces broken off from my heart at childhood. They are "alters" who represent the oppressive and negative feelings caused by the evil done to me. Both sides think, believe, and behave differently. I am living in two opposing worlds, one of good and the other of evil. The evil world is about negative feelings due to the demonic control, manipulation, and power I endured as a child.

There is a subtle shifting between logic and feeling. The analogy I see is a car with a stick shift. When you go from first gear to second gear, you immediately make the move, and both gears respond very differently. LOGIC/BELIEVING doesn't correlate to FEELING--two different sides, two different worlds.

Pastor Frank started asking me several questions. Since I was in my LOGIC/BELIEVING side, I was able to answer his questions rationally. Then Pastor Frank asked me something like, "How do you FEEL about that?" and I remember responding, "That's a deep question." I found myself unable to SWITCH from my LOGIC/BELIEVING side to answer this simple FEELING question. For me, LOGIC/BELIEVING and FEELING are separate worlds. I don't think it has always been like that.

I was still in my LOGIC/BELIEVING side when Jack started to pray. Sharon suddenly faded when my FEELING side and the alters took over with feeling sad, alone, fearful, and abandoned. When Dr. Jack used the word "crib," it all intensified:

> *Vague images came to me about being behind bars--was it a crib or a cage I was in? As a small child, THEY (the abusers) made me call and cry out to God, to mock God's non-response. Then someone representing Satan responded. Where was God? He didn't seem to have any power. Sherry, and the other alters were STUCK, BOUND, UNABLE TO MOVE.*

Later, when I made the switch back to Sharon, I would try to process what I heard Jack communicating. Basically I lived in my LOGIC/BELIEVING side until I was emotionally triggered.

My Body

When I reached 229 pounds, there were hardly any photos taken that would evidence the shame I felt. Healing my physical body from the unhealthy weight gain has been so hard for me. I told a close friend years ago, "I wish the Lord would have healed my body, before he healed my mind." My friend Alice reminded me that I was forgetting how bad my thought life really was.

I had to surrender to Jesus the hate I felt for my body. My hatred contradicted what Scripture said about my body being, "God's temple." I had to come to grips with the lies that kept me in bondage. I had to trust that God would change what bound my mind and heart. Jesus had understood betrayal first hand. Jesus understood what could be inflicted on one's body, what man had done to His body. What was needed was God's mercy and grace.

Though my pain and hate were directed at my body, I loved my spirit. I had used food to push down my shame and self-rejection. I used food to try to fill a hole that wouldn't go away.

My family knew nothing of my internal struggle. I isolated and kept my images, dreams, and flashbacks all that surfaced to myself. My husband knew nothing about the fears I lived with on a daily basis. He didn't believe that I was abused satanically by a cult. How could he? He later told me he knew something very bad had happened. I am grateful to my husband for his love and faithfulness throughout my healing process.

Moving South

After living in our home for almost thirty-five years, we decided to move south and start our retirement. I was happy for the warmer weather and for what was ahead. We would be moving into a new home not far from the ocean.

Inner Healing Ministry 2009

I found a church and signed up to take a course titled "Inner Healing." The second year I was asked to be part of the leadership team. Inner Healing was a powerful ministry. We met at my pastor's home every other week, and we would practice doing inner healing on each other. I was able to share several things from my past about sexual abuse.

During one of the nights we were meeting, the Pastor felt led to read to me the passage of "The Suffering Servant." **Isaiah 52:14 just as there were many who were appalled at him—his appearance was so disfigured beyond that of any man and his form marred beyond human likeness.** My Pastor said, "Jesus knows your pain, His outsides reflects your insides!" That Scripture and my Pastor's words helped me identify even more with what the Lord had been through. God's Word spoke loudly to me. Jesus understood all I had experienced.

A Response from the Father 2/16/11

Father God,
I still feel sick to my stomach. I drew a picture of a coffin and of a nail piercing into a heart. The words I wrote were "unwanted and hated". Lord, talk to me about this.
(Father God expressed these thoughts to me)
Dear Sharon,
Yes, Sharon, your childhood was very sad. There was very little for you to cling to, but that emptiness made you take hold of Me and My love for you. I have real protection for you because I AM in control, I have the power to protect you, and your family today. Your mother was putting the last nails in the coffin of your life, but I allowed them to put the LAST NAILS into my body to FREE YOU. I have conquered sin and death. I AM life, I AM your life. Nothing happens by accident. I AM summoning all that is in you that is not of Me to surface.
Love, Your Father

My Life Starts Falling Apart

It was in the late fall of 2015, out of nowhere, my life took a deep turn for the worst. There was nothing in my relationship with my husband or my daughters that was causing me concern. What I was facing was all internal, surfacing from my past.

I called places from one hour south of me to one hour north of me. I was crying while seeking help. The response was the same, "We can help you if you are addicted to drugs or alcohol." I told them I couldn't stop eating; that trauma was controlling me. They all said they couldn't help me.

I do not remember how I came across Dr. Roger's number, but I was able to make an appointment. I was drawn to him because he worked with what is called Dissociative Identity Disorder (DID) formally called Multiple Personality Disorder and Satanic Ritual Abuse. Before I met Dr. Roger, I sent him several papers I had written and several drawings as well. On our very first two hour appointment Roger told me that I had Dissociative Identity Disorder (Multiple Personality), and been through Satanic Ritual Abuse. Finally, I found someone who understood. I was in my late sixties, still trying to process what happened to me during the first ten years of my life.

I felt such peace in his office. My friend Connie came with me for almost every appointment and she took notes. Connie is a Christian psychiatric social worker. We laughed because we all called her the scribe. She was the cheapest scribe going; she spent the day with me, but she did get a free lunch.

I didn't know how my evil childhood events would surface. Little did I know that the Inner Healing ministry I took years earlier was going to be such a gift to me in the healing of my alters/ multiple personalities. Roger used prayer in all his sessions. Prayer would surface the demonic as well as the alters. Since I am writing about God's Story and understand very little about the demonic realm, I will trust that ministry to those who understand it. My book will focus on the Lord and the healing He brought me and my alters through prayer.

Chapter Two

PRINCESS, BLOBS, ANGEL AND LITTLE DANNY

11/19/15 Session with Roger

Roger opened in prayer and I tried to sense where the Holy Spirit was leading me. I visualized Sharon (adult), and Sherry (my inner child) walking down the hall into the Conference Room in my heart. One alter was there in a pretty dress. Roger told me to open the other door, and three smaller alters came inside. They couldn't get up on the chair, so they sat together on the floor. One was sucking her thumb. They appeared more like a "blob" than three small children.

Roger asked the girl what her name was and she said, "Princess." He replied, "That is a pretty name." Roger asked how old she was and she said, "Four." He asked what color her hair was, and she responded, "Long, they cut my hair; they took away my beauty!" He asked if they abused her, and she said, "Yes, but they dress me up like a princess!" Roger said he was sorry they abused her. Princess responds, "Destroyed! They dressed me up in a beautiful dress, and it was a lie and cover-up."

Roger asked Princess if she knew Jesus, Princess responded, "I only know lies."

Roger thanked the alters for coming and told them we wanted to help them.

Session 12/1/15 Conference Room in my Heart

11/19/15
Dear Princess, and the Blobs,

I thank all of you for coming to meet me. Princess, I am sorry you paid a price for being dressed up. I am sorry they lied to you. I hope you feel free to talk and tell us what you went through.

I want to teach you about Jesus and His love. They put a sword into his side. He suffered on the Cross with nails in His hands and feet. He did nothing wrong, but they killed him. Jesus understands the horrible things they did to you.

It was Jesus who wanted you to have the locket. It has a picture of you when you were four. You didn't have your pretty dress on. I put into the locket the Scripture Jesus gave me, **Psalm 107:20 He sent forth his Word, and healed THEM, He rescued them from the grave**. Jesus seeks to heal us. When you put your locket on, think of Him and think of me because I wore that locket everywhere. I am so happy Jesus gave it to you. It has a heart inside a heart. Remember I love you bunches.

Hello, little Blobs. I know you are too little to talk. I love you too. Thank you all for coming to the Conference Room. I hope you will continue to feel safe.

Love, Sharon and Sherry

12/1/15 Session with Roger

Roger started in prayer, and I visualized Sharon and Sherry walking down the hall holding hands; they are swinging their hands back and forth. Sharon is serious and focused, and Sherry is playful.

They enter the Conference Room in my heart and no one is there yet. After Roger's prayer I open the door and in comes Princess, three blobs, a girl, and a boy.

The girl talks first, and she says her name is "Nothing-Nobody." She tells us she is three years old, has long, blonde, curly hair and blue eyes. Roger wants to give her another name that isn't so negative and she responds, "Angel." Angel tells us she is not supposed to talk because she doesn't want to get hurt. Angel is defensive and fearful. She would shake in front of Bop (her grandfather).

The boy is "Little Danny." When he is asked his age, he holds up two fingers. Little Danny has short brown hair, a broken leg, about which he tells us, "They broke my leg!"

Angel is a seer; her eyes are illuminated. She sees everything. Angel saw them hurt Little Danny. Angel wants to stay quiet so the bad people don't hear and hurt her.

Angel has tears in her eyes. Roger asks if anyone wants to give her a hug. Sharon immediately jumps off the chair and Sherry follows. They both go and hug Angel. Angel says she can't remember ever being hugged.

Sherry takes Angel's hand, then takes Sharon's hand, and they make a circle and play ring-a-round the rosie. Princess and Little Danny want to play as well, so they leave the table and join in the circle. When they are all done playing, they pick up and carry the three blobs and go through the door.

12/3/15
Dear Angel, Little Danny, Princess, and the Blobs,

Thank you for coming to meet with Roger and me.

Angel, my heart goes out to you. I see your sadness, and your tears. I am sorry you have had to be silent all these years. I too had to bury my pain inside because there was no one who would understand it. The people who did bad things to us are dead and buried, and I would not let anyone hurt you again. I want you to share with me what was done to you that makes you afraid, shake and cry. It is sad to have no one there for you.

Angel, I am sorry you had named yourself Nothing-Nobody. Growing up, that is how people made me feel. Today, I know I am special and chosen because of Jesus. I no longer own what people said about me: I believe Jesus and what His Word says. I will help you understand Jesus' love for you.

I am not as playful as Sherry, especially when I am trying to focus on my troubled heart. My painful childhood memories have been blocked, and I cannot unblock them by myself.

When Sherry didn't trust Jesus, she still let Him pull her in a wagon. Then when she felt safer, Jesus played airplane with her. Today, Sherry can sit on His lap and feel the love and comfort He has for her. That is what I am praying for you.

Jesus' Word tells us in **Hebrews 4:13 Nothing in all creation is hidden from God's sight.** That means everything they did to you and the other alters, Jesus already knows. Jesus did not do bad things to you, the abusers did. They dressed up as Jesus to confuse, control, and manipulate you. They even told you Jesus does bad things to little children.

Angel, can you tell me what happened? I want you to know what it means to be protected and have the freedom to say whatever you need to break the silence and begin to heal your heart.
Love you bunches, Sharon

Little Danny, I am sorry they broke your leg. I can feel the anger in you, but you are a survivor and a fighter. I, too, am angry for what they did to you. I saw that Jesus healed your leg.

Little Danny, I have only vague memories of being in my grandfather's basement. I actually see a small child with a leg in a vice on my grandfather's work bench. Is that how they broke your leg? I see two people there. Was it my grandfather, and Uncle Carl that did this bad thing to you? I hope you can allow the memories to surface so healing can come, and then we can play and have fun.

Who told you that you had polio? That was a lie. That was to mislead you and cover-up what they did to your legs.

Little Danny, I want to help you, so please share about your pain and anger.

I am glad you and Princess came to play ring-a-round the rosie with us the other day. Playing is what little children should be doing.

Princess and the Blobs I want you to talk to me as well. I need words, thoughts, and memories. I need to hear your stories. Can you tell me about the bad things done to you?

Are there other alters inside me and do they want to talk?

I am sorry you were all small and vulnerable when you became shattered pieces of my heart. Jesus said in **Exodus 15:16B Your right hand O'Lord shattered the enemy**. God will shatter what the bad people did to hurt us. Jesus understands suffering, that they hurt us. . . and they tried to hinder us from remembering, so we couldn't get help. Help me by breaking the silence so we can heal.

Thank you for giving me your names; thank you for all the afflictions you carried for me so I was able to appreciate a loving and faithful husband and two wonderful daughters.

Let us become a loving and caring family together.

I love you bunches, Sharon and Sherry (the playful one)

Tears are coming down my cheeks and I hear the words, "I don't know what I did to deserve it?" Who is saying this? I hear, "Angel." Angel is sad; she is crying.

Angel, your tears are my tears. I am almost 69, and I still carry this pain from my childhood.

I read yesterday in **Joshua 6:1 Now Jericho was tightly shut up because of the Israelites. No one went out and no one came in.** Jericho was tightly shut up, and that is what I felt. Nothing can get in and nothing can get out.

I need your help Angel. I need to know what happened to you as a little girl. Jesus wants to free, comfort and heal us.

Is anyone else there with you? I hear, "Little Danny." I see Little Danny and Princess. They were like The Three Musketeers (Princess, Angel, and Little Danny). They huddle together. Princess, Angel, Little Danny, I thank you for being there for me. Can anyone help me to know more what is going on inside me?

Angel said, "They did bad things to us. They did bad things to my body." "Angel, what they did to your body they did to my body, but I can't remember anything."

Who remembers what they did to you? I hear three, "I do's."

So who wants to talk first? Who are the people who hurt you? Princess, I can see your hair is all chopped off. Who did that to you? Princess, your hair can be restored, and no one will ever chop it off again. Little Danny, they broke your leg. Do you remember who broke it? Little Danny, Jesus healed your leg so you can now play.

"Nana (my grandmother) cut my hair," said Princess. "Bop (my grandfather) broke my leg," said Little Danny.

Can you tell me more, Princess and Little Danny? Princess responds, "I was bad so they cut my hair." "So what did you do, Princess?" Princess answers, "Absolutely nothing."

BARRICADED AND SEALED

I could see them coming and I knew it meant trouble. Cars and trucks were coming from every direction – nobody could get near the house. The house was **BARRICADED** and the property surrounding the house looked like a used car lot.

I was in the three story house with my husband and another woman.

Every window was being **SEALED** shut so we could not escape. All the windows on the first floor were completely **SEALED** and they were working on the second floor.

The phone wires were cut, and all communication to the outside was impossible.

I was the only one that wanted to get out. I got dressed but didn't know how I would be able to escape without breaking my leg and jumping two stories.

1 Corinthians 10:13: **"No temptation has seized you except what is common to man. And God is faithful he will not let you be tempted beyond what you can bear. But when you are tempted, he will also provide A WAY OUT so that you can stand up under it."** 11/5/02

12/6/15 Awesome Sunday Communion Service

During the prayer before the Sunday worship service, I visualized three alters in a wagon. Jesus was pulling Princess, Angel and Little Danny in the wagon, and eventually they arrived at the ocean. They started playing in the sand with shovels that were already there. Jesus started making this large castle with a moat around it. Little Danny went to get water to put in the moat. That is where I left them.

Just before Communion I saw Jesus pulling the three kids in the wagon again. Jesus stopped the wagon in front of the Communion Table. Princess, Angel, and Little Danny got out. All three took Communion. When Communion was over, they got back in the wagon with Jesus, again pulling them. Awesome, awesome experience!

12/13/15 Sunday Afternoon Sharon is in Pain

I am very tired after church service. I am able to fall asleep, but I woke up in excruciating pain. The pain went down both my legs to my ankles. I tried to get up several times, but was unable to stand. Were the symptoms related to something in my past?

I asked the alters if they remember not being able to walk after leg pain? They offered no answer.

12/15/15 Session with Roger

Roger asked if anyone wanted to work on any concerns. As Roger prayed I close my eyes and I see Little Danny. He is two years old and he doesn't have words. I see him sitting on the floor with cars in both hands jamming them into his right leg. The left leg had been broken, but Danny is clearly banging the cars, which became big trucks, into his knees and shins.

Jesus got down on His knees and talked with Little Danny.

Princess is concerned that they chopped off her hair and took away her beauty. Roger asked Jesus to consider giving Princess back her hair. I see Jesus combing Princess's hair. The more Jesus combed her hair the longer it got! Her long, brown, wavy hair is now restored. Princess hugs Jesus; she is so happy that her hair is pretty again.

I see Angel looking at the coal chute in the basement. Angel is now in the basement and walking around. Angel says, "Someone put poop all over me." I did not tell this to Roger and Connie (my scribe) because I was embarrassed.

Princess, Angel, and Little Danny are back on my grandparent's living room floor playing.

In the kitchen there is a cold metal table, and I sensed something evil happened on that table.

12/17/15
Dear Lord,

I was thinking about Psalm 85 and the sermon, "Recovery, Life, and Death." Lord, what do I do with my damaged self? Lord, I am kneeling at the altar pouring out my heart to you, like Hannah. Hannah wanted a baby. I want a rebirth. I want to feel alive, I want to feel Your Presence.

They hurt Little Danny's small body. They broke his left leg and hurt his right leg. They told him he had polio. Who would do this to him?

Angel is in the basement and she is telling me they put poop all over her. Lord, I see a basement door. What is behind that door? What is this that happened to make Angel so sad? Send your angels to protect her so she can talk and share her pain.

Lord, who is coming up the back porch? Who is it I don't want to see? Who brings fear to Angel and me as well?

Princess, Angel, and Little Danny, I need your help in remembering.

Sherry (my inner child), I know you are always with me when I go into the Conference Room. What do you know? What do you remember? Are you trying to play all the time to cover up the pain that we carried? Can you help Angel and Little Danny remember? Angel is a seer, what would be a word to describe you? I hear the word "helper." Sherry can you help us now?

"Sherry, Princess, Angel and Little Danny can we meet in the Conference Room now?"

I see everyone has come around the table, and Jesus is there too. I don't like the table. Let's just sit in a circle on the floor near Jesus. Is this better? We can take turns sitting next to Jesus. Today, Princess and Angel, you sit next to him.   I see Danny climbing on His lap. Little Danny doesn't understand taking turns yet!

Lord Jesus, help us to remember.

I then think about the cold metal kitchen table. There is something evil that happened on it? What happened? Does anyone know?
Love, Sharon

12/20/15
Dear Princess, Angel, Little Danny,

Angel, I am sorry I didn't tell Roger what you said, that they put poop all over you. I do not want to silence you. Can you tell me who did that horrible thing to you?

Angel, I also sensed how afraid you are about someone coming up the stairs in the back of the house. I share your fear. I too, was afraid but I never knew why.

Angel, Jesus is with us today. He has many good angels who will watch over us. The people who abused you cannot confuse Him. He is God. He is awesome! Jesus takes our pain and fear away and redeems us.

Little Danny, I am sorry they hurt your legs. Thank you for showing me your pain through the play cars and trucks jamming your leg. Who did these bad things to you? Who hurt your legs? Jesus has healed them. I see you running to get water at the ocean for your pail. I love you Little Danny. You are a brave little boy.

I see Princess happy to have her beautiful hair back. Jesus knows exactly what you needed. He restored your beauty.

Well, kids, I am going to bed. It is very late.
Love all of you bunches, Sharon

Saturday 4:46 AM
Dear Princess, Angel, Little Danny, & Sherry,

Tears are falling from my eyes. I feel like I am carrying the weight of the world, in my body. I struggle with compulsive eating. Someone or something has taken over me to sabotage me, destroy me. Eating abnormally has been more of a problem since my childhood trauma began to surface.

Can anyone out there help me? I know you were told not to talk but could somebody sing out or write to me about what is going on inside?

Sherry singing: I was only a shell of a person. Food was my only comfort. I was empty and alone. I was never safe. I was hollow inside. They took everything, and left me as a Nothing-Nobody.

Sherry singing for Angel: Tears are all I really have. I am a Nothing-Nobody. I hate having a body. I hate what they did to my body. I want to die.   Angel says, "I am their piece of poop." They put poop over my naked body and make me dirty and I now stink. I hate this life. I want

I woke several times during the night. The first time I woke I heard,

"I AM NOT SUPPOSED TO TALK!"

"SO MANY EYES"

THEY ARE WATCHING ME?

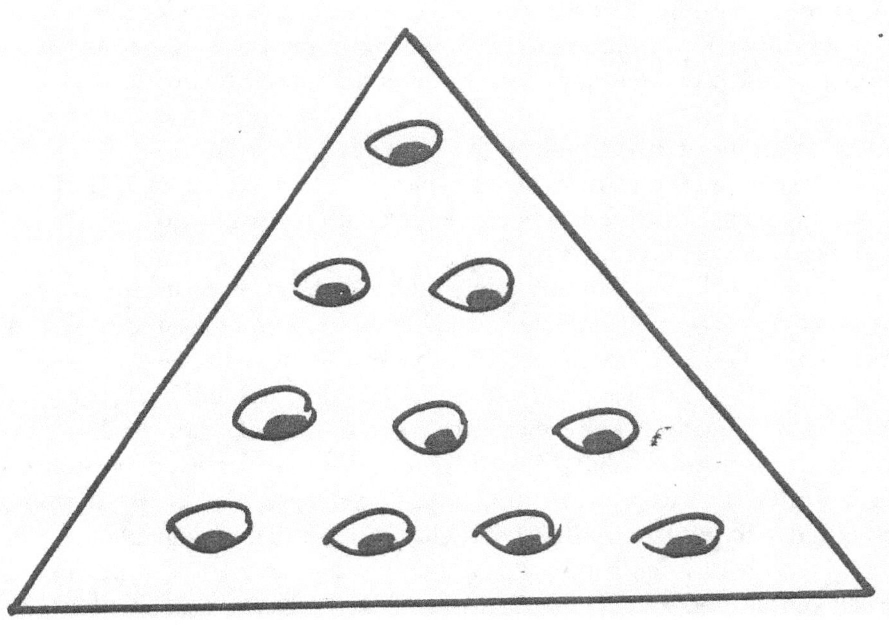

I had no feelings as I sat, at the kitchen table, drawing this new image. I started to think of the eyes which were part of my "safety net" and the people who were choosing to support me in this difficult journey. Immediately my thoughts went to 2 Chronicles 16:9 – "For the EYES of the Lord range throughout the earth to strengthen those whose hearts are fully committed to him."

to die. I am so sad. They wouldn't let me cry, so I cry on the inside where no one sees my tears.

Sherry singing for Little Danny: I hate them. I am little and they are bad. They hurt my legs so I would not talk. But they never said I can't sing. They are stupid!

Sherry singing for Princess: I hate when they buy me a dress. It is a lie. Outside pretty and inside destroyed. There is nothing inside but evil controlling my every move. I can't get out of line because they are watching. Life is hell inside. I want to be dead. They tried to drown us. I used to try holding my breath so I would die, and it would be over. No one cared that I am a little girl. My feelings were gone. I became their puppet. They pull the strings, and I move. I am their trash.

1/12/16 Session with Roger

Sometimes it is difficult to believe I am a victim of DID-SRA. Such a big part of my life has been blessed with my marriage to Dave and with my daughters and their families.

I asked Roger why my alters address me instead of him, making me a middle man. He explained that they hesitate to talk directly to him, because people have hurt them. They have an issue with trust.

I spoke with Roger about fortified cities, which have bars and gates, which relates to this Scripture that the Lord impressed on my heart: **Deuteronomy 3:5 All these cities were fortified with high walls and with gates and bars, and there were also a great many unwalled villages.** I told Roger I felt I had a walled city inside me. He related it to a hospital room with a dividing curtain. I told him mine is more complicated and fortified. Roger talked about a lady in Montana, that God's light was penetrating her walls. I felt like mine were thick impenetrable castle walls.

I told Roger when I was a little girl, they destroyed my body, but Roger told Angel that Sharon still has a body, and she could integrate back into Sharon's heart. Once the alters accept Jesus they can be one with Jesus in Sharon's heart. Someone asked what would happen to their pain. Roger explained the Lord heals the pain before you integrate. Roger said, "The best thing would be to integrate and strengthen Sharon, making her complete and whole."

Roger asked if Angel wanted to integrate, and she replied, "I need to ask Princess and Little Danny first. We are The Three Musketeers."

All were concerned about the three blobs as well. We all went back into the Conference Room in my heart. They are all going to integrate together, including the blobs.

Jesus gives Angel, Princess, and Sherry necklaces with hearts on it. He gives Little Danny a necklace with a truck on it. I can see Danny rocking the blobs in a cradle on the floor. They have resolved their pain; they are all safe and not alone anymore. EVERYONE IS NOW INTEGRATED.

1/22/16 Friday 3:23 PM
Father God,

As I continue to read from my old diary, I am struck by a video I watched on 4/28/02 using the Scripture, "in all things give thanks." There was nothing in my feelings that wanted me to do this, but I made a choice to obey this Scripture. **1 Thessalonians 5:18 Be joyful always, pray continually give thanks in all circumstances, for this is God's will for you in Christ**

Last week I had read in a book, "You don't give thanks for the ugly things, do you? You give thanks for the good things. But the Bible said, in all circumstances."

- Thank you Lord that you are continually revealing all that is not of You
- Thank you that You are Light and my darkness is constantly before You
- Thank you Lord that "nothing is hidden from Your sight," this includes everything done to me in secret
- Thank you Lord that there, "is nothing new under the sun"
- Thank you that there is more help today for those who suffer with DID-SRA
- Thank you for the way Your Spirit guides me into all truth
- Thank you that You put Roger into my path and gave me Connie for a scribe
- Thank you for the way You allow me to see images, visions and dreams
- Thank you for healing and integrating Princess, Angel, Little Danny and the Blobs

- Thank you that I hear in the Spirit, and as I get deeper into the evil, turn up my hearing Lord
- Thank you Lord, You have victory over evil, and You will have the last word
- Thank you for the way my alters communicate to both You and me
- Thank you Jesus for bringing The Three Musketeers to church for Communion -- it was an awesome experience
- Thank you for ordering my steps.
- Thank you for blessing me with faith, and, in all the darkness that surrounds my life, I know You already have won the victory
- Thank you for all that remains unhealed in me and for faith to overcome and see Your Glory
- Thank you that what feels like a fortified city inside me with bars and gates is nothing for You
- Thank you Lord that you created all things, and You know how to dismantle all that is not of You
- Thank you that I am sealed in You - I break any vows which marked me years ago against my will
- Thank you for keeping all this hidden, until I could handle it spiritually and emotionally in Your Name
- Thank you for a wonderful life with my family

Chapter Three

PUPPET (Danny), DOLLY, ANNIE, FOUR LITTLE ONES

1/25/16 Monday 11:07 AM
Father God,

I need you to bring your light to the dark trauma in me. Thank you that you have the power to bring back life, even raise the dead. Give me a life of freedom and wholeness by restoring and redeeming my alters.

Take back what the abusers have stolen from me. I lift up the parts of me that are still being held by Satan; asking you to sever those ties.

I give thanks that you are all powerful and all knowing. I thank you for the faith you have blessed me with. Give Roger wisdom. Give him eyes to see and ears to hear you Lord. Thank you for Connie's faithfulness as my scribe.

I pray tomorrow that I will see your power and glory at work in my session with Roger.
Love Sharon

1/26/16 Session with Roger

I shared with Roger about how I was convicted to give thanks in all things in a Bible Study. It is my choice to live this in obedience. So I spent time with the Lord writing down all that I was thankful for despite all I suffered from the abuse.

There was no new contacts with any alters during the past two weeks.

I asked about generational curses. Roger talked about sins of the occult being part of generational curses learned and passed on from childhood.

I talked about Bop and his case of liquor in the porch and how he howled like a madman for days. Alcohol and food addictions of my grandfather had passed down to my mother and also my siblings. I became a compulsive overeater trying to cope with what was suppressed and not yet healed.

We were in prayer when I had thoughts about Bop's black robe and cane. I saw a cage during prayer as well. Roger told me to open my eyes, and I told him about the cage. I told him I had thoughts of being on all fours with a cane around my neck, like I was a dog. He stated that was a common satanic practice.

Roger prayed again, and then I saw a person at the bottom of the steps.

Roger asked, "Are you an alter?" The alter answered, "I am a nothing, I am a puppet." Roger asked, "Do you have a name, and how old are you?" The alter replied, "Puppet and I am seven." Roger continued, "Are you a boy or a girl, and have you taken any abuse or trauma for Sharon?" Puppet replied, "I am a boy, and they hurt my body." Roger asked if he wanted a new name. Puppet says he has one, but it doesn't describe him. Roger told Puppet that he is special, and we wanted to call him by a name. Puppet said, "Everything was taken from me, even my name." Roger asked if there was something he would like to change. Puppet replied, "I have this wooden face with the body of a puppet."

Roger asked Jesus to bless this alter so he is able to feel love. He was resisting Jesus; he trusts no one. Roger told him the abuse is over now, and he is safe. Puppet replied, "I don't know what safe is."

I tell Roger I see Jesus and Puppet walk up the stairs, and there is a wagon. Puppet gets into the wagon, and Jesus pulls him to the ocean. Jesus often plays in the sand. Puppet says, "I do not know what play is." I start crying because I feel his misery. Tears!

I see Jesus stand up and cut the strings off Puppet. Puppet collapses to the ground in a heap, and then Puppet says, "I feel like a garbage heap."

Puppet slips out that his real name is Danny, and Roger picks up on it. Puppet says, "If I don't have a body, then they cannot hurt me. I am not ready for another body." Puppet is aware he came out of a dungeon.

Roger says, "Jesus, it is up to You to guide him." Puppet gets up, managing to climb into the wagon, and Jesus takes him away.

1/28/16 Thursday 4:46 AM
Dear Puppet,

I cried when I heard about your pain on Tuesday. I am so sorry you lived in a dungeon. Puppet, I want to help you. I know you are with Jesus somewhere.

Puppet I know your name is Danny, because you let it slip out three times. Maybe they took your name away from you, but I want you to have your name back. I want to call you Danny from now on. I hope that is okay with you.

I know you don't feel special or safe, and I know they didn't let you play. Well, their time is done, and I am going to teach you many things.

Psalm 16 teaches us about refuge, safety, and security. I, too, didn't feel safe for so many years. It took a long time for me to gain trust in Jesus. **Psalm 16:1 Keep me safe, O God, for in you I take refuge.** I learned that Jesus was my hiding place, and in 1991 I wrote in my Bible, "I have passed over -- I am safe, I feel safe."

Jesus and I will teach you that your pain and your time in the dungeon has ended.

I had circled the words in **Psalm 16:9 my body will also rest secure,** and in the margin I put a question mark since that wasn't my experience yet with my body. Danny, I hope you can help me understand why I have struggled with my body.

Jesus took you to the ocean in the wagon. I saw you looking around at the children playing on the beach. Jesus was playing with the sand, and you were watching.

Jesus cut the strings which made you obey their every command. Jesus broke their power over you. I am sorry you fell into a heap. Danny, you are not garbage.

You are a strong and courageous boy who helped me more than you can understand. I pray that you will let Jesus restore you back into your body. You really don't have a wooden face and a puppet's body.

Little Danny had his leg broken when he was two years old and Jesus healed them. Now he loved being at the ocean making castles with Jesus. Little Danny would run to the ocean with a pail to get water. His leg was no longer broken. He loved to sit on Jesus' lap. Jesus and Little

Danny became good buddies. Puppet, I hope that restoration for you as well.

Danny, are there any other children locked in the dungeon? I can go get them with Jesus' help. The gate is gone, and the gatekeeper is locked up. You never have to go back there again. If there are other children there, we need to get them out.

Thank you Danny for protecting me all these years by carrying my trauma.

Love you bunches, Sharon

Friday 1/29/16
Dear Jesus,

Thank you for taking Danny out of the dungeon and to the ocean for healing.

Lord, he sees his body as that of a puppet. Somehow give him a new body and help him to see he is now safe from evil.

If he can't talk, can he sing? Just like Little Danny said, "They were stupid; they didn't say he couldn't sing.

If there are any other children stuck in the dungeon would you release them as well. Bring them out of what has confined them for years. Thank you Lord for taking away the gate and binding up the gatekeeper with the sentry.

Thank you that Danny saw you cut the strings, and free him from their ways. Help him to see he is not wooden. Restore to Danny all that was taken away. Cleanse him with your Word and give him words that speak to him. Give him a special Scripture that will speak to his broken heart. Make him whole Lord.

Love, Sharon

2/3/16
Father God,

I was thanking You for a wonderful family and yet started crying about my fragmented self.

My alters do not know what a family is. They only know separation and pain. Lord it hurts me to know that they have lived in a dungeon for almost seventy years. How miserable for alters to represent a shattered and fragmented parts of me. How depressing that they had to take on and carry my hurt and pain. Tears are rolling down my face.

Danny's sees himself as a puppet and even his name was stripped from him. His strings have now been cut, but having lived that way for so long, he can't see he is a boy. Lord, he doesn't want a body because he is afraid of more pain. Lord, I know he is in your Presence somewhere. Heal his wounded heart.

Give big Danny the strength to accept his liberated self. He is not supposed to talk, so give him the ability to communicate another way. The evil people have not won -- help Danny to see that.

I pray you would have Danny let us know who else is in the dungeon. We need his help.
Love, Sharon

2/8/16 Session with Roger

Roger asked how I think my alter Danny is doing, and I don't know. I have cried some since our last session and wrote prayers to Jesus to get me to deal with what needed healing.

Connie, my scribe, asked me if I feel more peace or more turmoil now. I am seeing God's power heal the alters, but also am aware that digging deeper means meeting more evil and terror.

As Roger prayed for wisdom and protection. I see myself looking down the steps into the dungeon, seeing an abyss, with terror in its depths.

I see a light down at the bottom of the steps. Maybe it is Jesus' light.

I see a little girl as she approaches the stairs; she is confused. She does not know what light is; she only knows darkness. Jesus helps her up the stairs and out of the darkness. She has a dress on. She doesn't have a face! She reminds me of an image I had of four paper dolls in which a finger erased all the faces.

Roger prays for the alters. I see Jesus giving her a face! Jesus has given her eyes, which she tries to keep closed. Jesus puts a beautiful purple flower up to her nose. She opens her eyes to see what smells so good.

Jesus is aware she is afraid of the dungeon. He walks her away and they are in a meadow. She and Jesus pick flowers; she has a bouquet of them.

She reveals she has a hole in the center of her being, which reminds me of, "Emptiness the Hole." Roger asks Jesus to do something with the hole. I see Jesus with a flashlight looking around and through the hole. Jesus starts stitching up the opening.

Roger asks her name and age. She said, "Call me Dolly, I am five."

Jesus and Sharon leave the meadow and go back to the dungeon. There are four more alters on the steps. They are smaller than Dolly, and they have a connection to the paper dolls. When they see Dolly, they run over to her.

Jesus gets a wagon, and Dolly puts them in, pulling the wagon to follow Jesus. As the sun goes down, they are getting afraid of the dark. It reminds them of the dungeon. They reach the cottage on the other side of the meadow, Jesus puts the light on, and they are not afraid.

Roger asks their names and their ages. They respond, "Three." Of the four, one is a boy alter.

Somebody says, "Where is Danny?" Danny comes out, and he is no longer a puppet; he looks like a normal boy.

The cottage living room is really bright, and Jesus is by the fireplace observing the interaction. Danny and Dolly are talking. Dolly no longer has a hole in her body; she also has her face back.   She can see, and hear again, and Danny is no longer a puppet. Jesus has healed them both.

Jesus is now on the rocking chair. Danny and Dolly are in the living room by the fire. Dolly fears she will have to go back to the dungeon. Danny says he will never have to go back and now lives in the cottage.

There is a Surrender Box in the middle of the floor, and Danny tells Dolly he surrendered his puppet outfit to Jesus, putting it in the box because he didn't need it anymore. Danny asks Dolly if she wants to put anything into the Surrender Box for Jesus. Dolly takes off a ring from her finger and surrenders it to the Box.

Danny said Jesus teaches him every night by the fireplace about Himself, convicting Danny to give his heart to Jesus. Dolly has given her ring up, but is not sure she wants to give up her heart.

The four new alters are called the "Four Little Ones." Dolly said she only has half a heart because the Four Little Ones broke her heart when they were beaten with bats.

The Four Little Ones are in the bathroom taking a bath. They are sliding down the back of the tub into the water. Tired out, the four of them go to sleep in one bed.

I now get an image that the Four Little Ones have the light on and are not sleeping. They are all jumping up and down on the bed. I start laughing at the image, while Roger is praying. I am hysterically laughing. My laughing goes on and on. I cannot stop. My face is becoming red. Roger and Connie want to know what was so funny. When I stopped laughing I shared with them what I was visualizing.

Roger said we need to go back to see if there are others to rescue. I think of the dungeon and I am aware of my fear of it.

Roger started to pray. Roger called for any alters that remain in the dungeon. There is one little girl hiding in the corner. Jesus helps her up the stairs. Her hair is dirty and ratty. She wants to hide, not wanting anyone to see her. Jesus turns the wagon into a covered wagon with a protective top, and Jesus takes her to the cottage. The Four Little Ones called her, "Annie." They take her in the bathroom for a bath. One of the Four Little Ones jumps into the tub with Annie. Later the five of them go into the bedroom. I see Annie bury herself under the covers so no one can see her. They all go to sleep. They are now safe.

I finally see the dungeon empty.

2/19/16
Father God,

Thank you Lord for restoring Dolly's face, and having her eyes open to see what smelled so good. Dolly still needs a new heart. Hers was broken when the Four Little Ones were hit with the bats. Lord, please give her a new heart or restore the one she has.

Dolly surrendered a ring to the Surrender Box where Danny put his puppet outfit. What does the ring represent? Why would a five year old have a ring and then choose to surrender it?

Thank you that Danny, Dolly, Four Little Ones, and Annie are safe with you at the cottage.

Thank you for a wonderful laugh with the scene of the Four Little Ones jumping on the bed.

Lord, why is Annie hiding? You put her in a covered wagon because she needed that protective space. Annie has now buried herself under the blankets so she can't be seen. What trauma caused this?

I pray that you will fully restore the alters that are now living in the cottage with you. I pray you will give them words to expose and then heal all that is bound in them.

I pray, Father God, that they would see Your love and accept You in their hearts.
Love, Sharon

Dear Danny, Dolly, Little Ones, and Annie,

Dolly, I am so sorry that you were like a faceless paper doll. You were afraid to be able to see, hear, and even talk. I am happy Jesus restored your face, and you are now living in the cottage with everyone.

I am sad for what the ring represented to you, and that you had only half a heart. I know Jesus will fix your heart and restore all that was taken away from you and the Four Little Ones.

Four Little Ones, thank you for making me laugh so hard. I loved seeing you jump on the bed. I loved seeing you use the back of the tub as a slide. When Annie was taking a bath I know one of you jumped into the tub. Thank you for doing that for Annie. I pray that you will all find the words so you can tell your stories.

Annie, my heart breaks for all you suffered. I hope you can come out from under the covers and go be with everyone in the living room. Jesus rescued you from the dungeon forever.

Annie, Jesus loves little children. You were given a covered wagon because He knew you were afraid.

Danny, Dolly, Little Ones, and Annie, I pray that you will spend your days getting to know Jesus and letting him bless your life.

I love you all so very much.

Love, Sharon

2/23/16 Session with Roger

As I revisited my traumatic childhood, I could feel an ache in my chest. The pain became more intense as the session went on. I believe it was Dolly's pain regarding her broken heart and what the Four Little Ones experienced.

Annie has been so afraid. It has slipped out that Annie didn't know or believe in Jesus, but when Jesus came with the covered wagon Annie immediately got into it.

The scene changes, and Jesus and Annie are in a meadow. Annie sees Danny, Dolly, and the Four Little Ones playing with the animals and picking flowers in the meadow.

Jesus is sitting on a big rock. Dolly goes over to the rock, sits down and starts talking to Jesus. "If you are God, why did you let them hurt the Four Little Ones?" Jesus starts telling about the Father's love and how He watched Jesus suffer. Jesus was trying to connect Dolly with what the Father had gone through. Jesus talks about the evil He had endured and that He chose to go through it. He talked about the nails in His body, that He suffered, died, and conquered death. Jesus expresses sorrow that Dolly and the Four Little Ones suffered and that she only had half a heart.

Danny has been telling Dolly how he surrendered his heart. Jesus heals Dolly's heart, and it enlarges into a big heart. Now she now wants to surrender her heart to Jesus as well.

Danny comes over to the rock by Jesus and Dolly. Danny and Dolly now have both given their hearts to Jesus. Annie is in hearing distance and she says, "I'm not giving my heart to anyone! I don't even know if I have a heart to give. I am hollow, empty, like a shell washed up on a beach."

The Four Little Ones have now joined everyone on the rock. They are sitting on Jesus' lap. Annie is near the rock but will not join Jesus and the others. Roger tells me to trust that she will be taught like the others.

Jesus walks around Annie with scissors and cuts off all the invisible strings attaching her to evil. Annie falls over in a heap, just like Danny, when Jesus cut off the strings to his puppet costume. Jesus picks her up and puts her in the covered wagon where she will feel safe.

Everyone sitting on the rock is singing, "Jesus loves me, this I know, for the Bible tells me so."

The Surrender Box from the cottage appears and is now near the rock. The box now contains Danny's puppet outfit, Dolly's ring, and now the Little Ones want to put their smashed hearts in the box as well. They put their damaged hearts in the box as Jesus gives them four new hearts. Annie pulls out what was left of the strings that controlled her and puts them in the box. Annie has gone from exhausted to relieved, yet she still does not want to join everybody on the rock.

The Four Little Ones go over to join Annie in the covered wagon.

There is laughter going on. The Four Little Ones are funny. I see them jumping up and down on the top of the covered wagon, and they suddenly break through the top. Annie has now lost her covering, but she doesn't care. The Four Little Ones try to tell Annie about their new hearts. But Annie has nothing inside. Even if she got a heart it would fall to her feet because she is empty. Jesus tells her He would put her heart back in with "silly putty."

Annie and the Little Ones are in the uncovered wagon with their new hearts. Annie is exhausted but happy to be with the Four Little Ones.

Jesus gets the wagon, and they all squeeze on and still are able to play. They want to go back to the cottage. They are hungry and want to eat. Jesus brings the Surrender Box into the house and places it by the fireplace.

Jesus is at the table praying, and He thanks the Father for the cut strings, new hearts, and the covered wagon not being needed anymore.

He prays for Annie, her new heart, even the silly putty holding her heart in place, and that Annie's emptiness will be filled.

Annie and the Four Little Ones eat and go to bed. Annie lays at the center of the Four Little Ones. She is no longer hiding under the blankets. Danny and Dolly are still with Jesus at the kitchen table.

Roger said to me, "You may never fully know what happened to the alters. You know Jesus healed them. It's all about Jesus."

2/29/16
Dear Jesus, Danny, Dolly, Little Ones, and Annie,

Danny and Dolly, I am so grateful that you both have surrendered your hearts to Jesus.

Dolly, I saw that Jesus replaced your broken heart with a new big heart. Your big heart will hold all the love you have always had for the Four Little Ones. The pain of your broken heart was the pain I felt during my therapy session. My pain went away when Jesus replaced your broken heart with the new big heart.

Jesus, when you sat on the big rock in the meadow, I thought immediately about you being "The Rock." Thank you for that image. Thank you that Danny and Dolly chose to be with You, and Dolly shared her pain-filled heart with you. Thank you for the care You took with Dolly's questions. Thank you for restoring Dolly's heart and that both Danny and Dolly gave their hearts to you.

The Four Little Ones are just like Little Danny. They just want to climb up and sit on Your lap. Thank you for restoring their hearts as well.

Annie, you have come a long way. Jesus knew exactly what you needed, and He gave you a covered-wagon. Do you know you are the only alter that Jesus did that for? That is because He knew exactly what would make you feel safe.

Annie, did you laugh a little when the Four Little Ones damaged the covered-wagon? Well, they really made me laugh, you didn't need a covering anymore.

Annie, I saw you tucked in bed in the center of the Four Little Ones. You no longer had a need to hide under the covers. Isn't this your own new family now? Jesus is light; Jesus delivered all of you from the dungeon. Jesus loves all of you so very much.

Four Little Ones and Annie, I need to ask all of you a question. "Are you ready to allow Jesus to come into your new hearts?" Jesus wants to guide and protect you. Jesus does that by living inside us, but we have to invite Him in. We have to open the door to our hearts. Is there anybody willing to do that? Who wants to be first?

I see you all sitting in a circle, and all five of you have raised your hands.

So repeat after me: "Jesus come into my heart. I know sometimes I do bad things, and I need you to forgive me and save me. I am sorry for doing wrong. I accept you as my Lord and Savior; come and live in my heart." Now you can all close the door of your hearts where Jesus entered, because Jesus is now living in your hearts.

The next question is, who wants to come and live in me? Danny, Dolly, Four Little Ones and Annie, you are parts of me that split off many years ago. It is like I am a puzzle and you are my missing pieces.

Princess, Little Danny, Angel, and the Blobs are already part of me.

I need your help because, the stronger I am, the more I can go back and help the others who are still living in darkness. So, would you like to join me and be together like one big family? Line up like they do at school if you want to be with all the others.

I am proud of you Annie, you beat the Four Little Ones getting in line! I don't know how Jesus will do it, but He will INTEGRATE us and make us all family. We will all be sealed in Jesus. We can now go as one with Jesus and rescue all the other alters who are in the darkness. You can all help me.

I love you bunches, Sharon

Chapter Four

**MISCHIEF, BUTCH, NO-NAME (Annie), CANDY,
THE EIGHT LITTLE ONES**

3/8/16 Session with Roger

I was curious about the comment that Roger made last time we met, "Your alters may not have surfaced all they went through when they rejoin and integrate with your heart."

Roger suggests I visualize the Conference Room and we meet there in my heart. Thoughts about clothes in the back of a closet came to mind. As I prayed, I gave the Lord permission to move anything hidden in the back of the closet to the front.

I can see the Conference Room, and this time I am alone. Sherry is not with me. I am opening one of the doors, and there are a slew of alters inside. I see four main alters. Roger asked the main alters to come in. They sat at a table with two on one side and across are the other two.

Roger asked me to focus on one of the alters. Her name is No-Name and she is five years old. She has brown hair and eyes and is wearing a dress. No-Name says, "I took a lot of trauma for Sharon, why am I here?" She does not know who Jesus is.

The next alter's name is Mischief and she is also five. She has shorts on, red hair, and hazel eyes. She was asked if she took trauma for Sharon and replied, "They hurt me. I hate them and I am not supposed to talk."

Butch is a boy alter who is five and has blonde hair and blue eyes. When asked if he took trauma for Sharon, he responded, "That's all I have known. Is this a jail?" Roger tells him we want to help him get out of bondage.

I focus on the last alter. Her name is Candy.   She is six and has a mask over her eyes. Candy doesn't want to see or be seen. She is asked if she suffered trauma for Sharon and responds, "Are you going to hurt me too?" Roger tells her that she is safe and that we would never hurt her. Candy responded, "They kicked me. I hated being there, even being alive. I hate what they did!"

Candy is the oldest of the alters. She said they gave her a sweet name, but there was nothing sweet about her. "It is all a lie." Roger tells her, in spite of what they did to you, you are still sweet.

Mischief is now sitting on the table. She said, "When I am not tied down, I do my own thing." The others are trying to get Mischief off the table, because they have always paid for her acting out.

They all want to know where they are going when they leave the Conference Room. They are told they can stay there if they feel safer. Butch said, "It would be better than where we came from."

Roger asks the Lord to provide for their needs, to make them safe and secure. A sentry is placed at the door.

Someone asks if the Eight Little Ones outside can come in. They come in and sit on the floor in a circle.

Butch wants to know who was standing in front of the other doors. Roger said, "They are warrior angels."

It feels like kindergarten; everyone is on the floor with a mat and a pillow eating cookies. Mischief is up on the table again with her mat and a pillow. She doesn't do what everyone else does.

Sharon is on the floor asking questions, and No-Name said, "You will get nothing out of me."

Mischief is on the table, and she said, "I'll talk." Mischief took off her clothes, put them in a pile, and said, "They tied me down like this." I could visualize Mischief on the table naked with her arms and legs stretched out to all four corners. The others are still trying to get Mischief back on the floor. Then someone was calling Mischief, "wicked." The others are mad at her because she is going to get them in trouble.

Roger told them not to be mad, because they will no longer get into trouble. Then Mischief spoke, "They gave me something to drink and I saw cloudy." Roger asks if she sees cloudy now. Mischief replied, "When I try to remember…it is hard to make out faces."

The Eight Little Ones are all in the corner and playing Simon-Sez. They do as they are told; they follow their leader, Mischief. They are all taking their clothes off in a circle, making a pile. They only know how to obey.

Mischief said, "You'll get nothing out of No-Name." When Mischief is asked her impression of No-Name, she said, "She is a nothing, helpless, and by avoiding a real name she believes she doesn't exist."

Roger asks the Lord to bless them with what they need.

The Eight Little Ones now have their clothes back on.

Mischief is asking the warrior angel at the door, "How did you get to be an angel?" The angel replied, "It is our job to help you." Butch is talking to the other angel. Butch looks like an angel, but he is not treated like one. Butch is throwing up in a bucket. Roger is praying for healing. I am reminded of the series, "The Sacrifice," done at church, and, afterwards, how I went home to vomit. Roger asks if Butch was involved in a sacrifice. He replied, "Just the word will make me sick." Roger asked me if there was a sermon I heard recently on sacrifice.

Roger said these alters may be close to remembering—they may have shared some of your recent bouts of throwing up. Sharon is trying to comfort Butch, and she was nauseous this week as well.

I felt guilty as I told Roger that it might be a book I read on SRA that made this alter sick. Roger suggested it was a good idea not to read those books to avoid memory triggers. I asked why triggers from reading about SRA are bad, but he did not give a response.

Mischief acts out, and Butch feels the others alters, No-Name and Candy, are useless.

Roger asked me how I feel about there being twelve more alters. I told Roger, "They all represent unhealed trauma but I feel 80-85% whole."

Roger talked about the fact that I used the name Sharon instead of "I" or "me." Roger asked me to ask the Lord's direction whether there is another alter sharing executive control of my core person.

3/10/16
Father God,

Thank you today for this beautiful, windy day. Thank you for the quiet and the peace within.

Lord, help me always to rest in you. Help me to still my soul and spirit. As I settle into this day, I thank you for so many blessings.

I want to find freedom in you. I want to connect all that is disconnected in me. I want to stop just surviving and thrive in you. I surrender all missing pieces/parts/alters that keep me from wholeness and health.

Father, help me to feel, help me to have normal God-given emotions that are part of living. You created me with feelings for a purpose. Restore the healthy, normal feelings they have stolen.

Lord, Roger had brought up something about Sharon sharing her core person. Help Roger and me to have clarity. Is Sharon sharing executive control with someone else?

Father, who is inside that cries? Restore the memories that I need to address to make me whole. The alters will never make me whole unless You guide their healing and integration.

I pray you will fill me with your Holy Spirit. Fill me to overflowing, Lord.

I have felt stuck and dead inside. Thank you that you have a plan to deliver me, just like you did for the Israelites at the Red Sea.

Thank you for the many ways you are taking care of the issues of each hurting part within me. Thank you for teaching my alters all about you, your love, and your care for them.

Thank you that you know everything the abusers did to me. Thank you for all the tears you shed for me.

Lord, you rose Lazarus from the grave. Help me trust that you will raise what is dead in me. Thank you that when you speak the Word, that it shall happen, not before, but in your timing.

The whole process of being able to visualize alters who surface my hidden trauma in prayer still amazes me. I am sorry for my unbelief that not enough will be remembered to be healed.

Well, Lord we now have a slew of alters. No-Name didn't want her name changed. Mischief and Butch seem to be the alters that were sharing the most. Candy seemed content that she has a mask on.

Lord, why did Mischief say, "When I am not tied down, I do my own thing?" Lord, who tied her down? When Mischief got up on the table, the others were trying to get her back on the floor. Why did Mischief take her clothes off and stretch her arms and legs to each corner of the table? What did they give Mischief to drink that clouded her mind? I pray that you would take the clouds away from Mischief so she can remember. Restore her vision so she can see all that you need her to see. If she needs to know their faces, make them clear.

Thank you for the two warrior angels guarding the Conference Room.

Butch looks angelic, but he isn't treated like an angel. Lord, why is he throwing up in a bucket? Was I sensing his pain last week when my stomach was upset for days?

Butch had said, "Just the word sacrifice would make him sick."

I am aware that Mischief acts out and Butch is a feeler. Lord, help me understand their needs.

Lord, Why are there Eight Little Ones? What is their purpose? They were playing Simon-Sez, and then they took off their clothes. They are so little; what was done to them?

Lord, surface what needs to be revealed for Your healing of my life.

I give you everything that came up yesterday, and I will focus on You in the deliverance of my shattered self.

Love, Sharon

Father God's Reply to Me
Dear Sharon,

Be still and know that I am God. In quiet and rest my answers will come to you.

Just as those clouds are moving across the sky, I will move the clouds that are blocking Mischief's vision. She will know all that she needs to understand.

I have moved your alters closer to the surface, and you have another series of parts that need to be heard, loved, and healed.

They will be safe in the Conference Room of your heart. I will spend time there just as I did in the cottage. I will bring the alters toys and sand from the ocean, and the wagon will be there.

I will love on them and play with them. There will be a fireplace and rocking chairs so that I can read to them before bedtime.

The Surrender Box will be in the corner of the Conference Room.

Be still my child. Trust in me. Trust in the process.

Love, Your Daddy in Heaven

Saturday 3/12/16
Dear Mischief, Butch, No-Name, Candy, & Eight Little Ones,

I want to thank you all for coming to the Conference Room. I know you are all afraid of more trauma and you were always told not to talk. You will be hurt no longer.

Mischief, I am sorry for the tremendous pain that was inflicted on you. You said, "They had me take off all my clothes, get up on the table and tie me down, stretching out my arms and legs." You said they drugged you, and you saw "cloudy." You said it was hard to make out the faces. Can you tell me if this happened in Nana's kitchen? Do you have any idea who did this to you? Do you remember what they did? Can you talk or act out your pain? You need to tell your story to be free.

Jesus can tell you what cruel and evil things they did to Him. He was innocent, just like you, but they hurt him anyway. Maybe you can share your story with Him. Whenever you want to speak or show me something, I will listen. When I wrote to Jesus yesterday, He told me He would remove the clouds that are blocking your memory.

Butch, I am sorry you took the trauma for me. You looked like an angel but were hardly treated like one. I could see you throwing up in a bucket. Maybe what I was reading caused you to feel sick. I am sorry that the word "sacrifice" triggers so much discomfort in you. Jesus is with you now, and the bad people have passed away. Jesus chose to suffer and be a sacrifice so that all could be free. Maybe He can share with you the pain He went through with all the evil that was done to Him. Someone said that you are the feeler. Well, could you share what you feel inside? I feel nothing because you took the "feelings" for me. You can keep vomiting, but that will never free you. Help me understand what was done to you.

No-Name, I am sorry that you don't even want a real name, because it is easier for you to act like you don't exist. You will keep your pain inside by pretending you don't exist. You will have to stop pretending and confront your hurt. You need to put words to your pain so we can help you. I would like you to have another name so being without a name doesn't define you. Is there another name we can call you that you might like?

Candy, I am sorry you feel you need a mask on so that you can't see what had happened to you or anyone else. Pretending doesn't make the pain go away. You have a sweet name, and we want to restore all your sweetness back to you. I want you to feel safe and be able to take off your mask. The bad guys told you not to talk, because they knew talking would be freeing. What part have you played to become a missing piece for me?

Eight Little Ones, I am sorry what was done to you, using the game Simon-Sez for bad reasons. You will not be hurt any longer. You will not have to take your clothes off. Why are there eight of you? Jesus loves little children. He wants to heal you. Do you have words; can you communicate your pain?

Jesus, you are with all my "alters" in the Conference Room. You know what each of them needs to do and say to be healed and free. Help them to be free of the terror they had experienced.

I love You Father so much for caring for each and every part of my divided self.
Love, Sharon

4/3/16
Father God,

Yesterday, I really had to think about the question that came up in my women's therapy group: "Do you feel too wounded to heal?" I was envious of some of the women's ability to remember the circumstances of their pain and be able to tell their stories.

I had little inside, numb feelings, hardly anything to work with—little ability to even recall the abuse. Now I can just sit, wait, and trust You to enable the trauma to surface, what I need to know and overcome.

There are no pictures of me as a newborn or as a small child. However, I have a vague sense someone was taking pictures during my abuse.

Did I come into the world to be destroyed by wicked people, to feel no love, no value, no meaning to my being born, but to be used for evil purposes.

For years I hated my body, but I never understood why I felt so unlovable, and I believed that there was something really wrong with me.

I remember being extremely afraid of my grandfather, but I had no memory of what he did to me to cause my fear. My memory was taken from me, just like my innocence.

My mother had told me that my father didn't want me, and then told me neither did she! What does a little girl do with all that rejection? I learned to exist by being empty inside.

I had no one to go to in the night when I was hurt or afraid as a child. I had no one to go to during the day, either.

As I now seek healing from the abuse, I feel so alone. I am getting some images, but basically it's a struggle to gain any recall.

How do I heal, Lord? How do I connect the images that I have to address, reveal, to heal the traumatized little girl within? It is almost like my childhood hardly existed.
Love, Sharon

Father God's Reply
Dear Sharon,

I created you in your mother's womb; you are my child. I cared for my Creation so much that I let my Son die, so that you could choose the life I envisioned. Evil was allowed to take my Son's life for My purpose, and evil took a part of your life too.

I know you feel stuck, dead inside.

The Israelites felt stuck and trapped at the Red Sea. I had a plan to deliver them. I led them to a dead-end, and it was there that they found Me. You will find Me in your dead-end as well. Someday you will look back on your deliverance and marvel at all I did.

Annie needed a covered-wagon and do you think I don't know your needs? I remember everything they did to you. I remember everything they did to my Son. I wept for both of you. I weep for all my Creation.

I will restore what the locusts have eaten. I will restore all that is unconnected, lost and lifeless. You will thrive in Me in a way beyond your comprehension.

I know everyone of your parts that remains in the darkness. They are neither trapped nor stuck. Your trauma will unfold like a rose. I am not only unfolding your past, I am unfolding your future. **Let's call it, "Deliverance to Destiny."**

I will teach you many things. These are lessons not just for you, but for you to teach and heal others.

I can call memories forth, just like I called Lazarus from the grave. I will call them out of the darkness, and when I speak, life will come.

Do not focus on what you think you need. Focus on Jesus who came to save you. Focus on My love. Focus on My power, and focus on Me as your Redeemer and King.

Love, Your Daddy

4/5/16 Session with Roger

My ailing back, physical therapy treatments and upper respiratory problems, involving visits to three different doctors, had taken a toll.

In the beginning of the session, I gave both Roger and Connie copies of the picture I had drawn and two letters, one to the Lord and the other to the alters, I had written after my last session.

The picture showed three different scenes discussed during my last visit with Roger. I am in the Conference Room sitting at the table with Mischief, Butch, No-Name and Candy (with her mask on). There

4/5/16
Candy
Annie-
NoName
Door
Door
Warrior
Angels
Sharon
Butch
Mischief
Eight Little Ones
Naked clothes in a pile
playing simon-sez
Mischief
Naked on the table
clothes in a pile
"When I am not tied
down, I do my own thing."
"They gave me something to
drink + I see cloudy: when I
try to remember... it is hard
to see faces"

were two Warrior Angels guarding both doors. To the right of the table there were the Eight Little Ones who were naked, their clothes in a pile, playing Simon-Sez. On the bottom I drew Mischief lying on the table naked, her clothes in a pile, and her hands and legs stretching to the table corners.

Mischief had said, "When I am not tied down, I do my own thing. They would give me something to drink and I see cloudy. When I try to remember…it is hard to make out faces."

As Roger read my letters he commented about the alter No-Name and other past issues in my therapy. He said, "If you were abused by a doctor, your alters would then not trust a doctor."

Roger referred to my question of why he had chosen to go back to the Conference Room rather than the dungeon. He said, "I presume it was the Lord that gave me that direction. We need now to head back to the Conference Room." Roger began praying to the Wonderful Counselor.

I could see in my mind the Conference Room. Jesus has brought many things from the cottage and the ocean—sand, the red wagon, rocking chairs, the fireplace, toys, and the Surrender Box, which was placed in the corner of the room. I can see Jesus sitting in a rocking chair with the two Warrior Angels at the door. The Eight Little Ones are playing in the corner of the room, and I am sitting around the table with Mischief, Butch, No-Name, and Candy.

Jesus left the rocking chair and sat down at the table. Jesus asked, "Does anyone want to talk?" No-Name and Candy said, "No, not me." I got up and walked over to Candy because I could identify with her and the mask that was covering her eyes. I told her, "There is a part of me that doesn't want to see either." As I spoke, tears were coming down my face. Roger asked, "Why don't you and Candy want to see?" I said something like, "It has been difficult dealing with the evil done to us." I felt Candy's pain because it was my pain.

Then Candy took off her mask and set it on the Conference table! "Candy, I am really proud of you. I will be right back because I needed to go and talk with No-Name who I also identified with."

I told No-Name that my name was confused when I was little, and I think the mistake on my birth certificate was done on purpose. I told No-Name that I was not sure who my father was, and possibly it was my grandfather Bop. Roger then asked me, "Who did your mother say was your biological father?" I replied, "My mother said Lola and I both had the same father."

I was aware my mother was promiscuous and had several abortions when she was young. My mother didn't like any of her children, but I was the one she really hated. The child she had after me she gave up for adoption. My mother's history suggested she may have been a victim of sexual abuse.

While pursuing if No-Name wanted to have a new name, she responded, "Just call me Annie." No-Name had a real name now, though there was another alter named Annie.

Annie went over and sat next to Candy. Mischief and Butch are sitting together and have remained quiet up until now. I asked the group, "Who would like to talk?" Butch said, "I am the feeler, that is my role, and Mischief's is to act out."

I asked Mischief if she has trouble acting out, and she said, "I don't have emotion and just act out."

I ask, "Does anyone want to share your story?" I reminded them that, "No-Name changed her name, and Candy had already removed her mask."

Mischief said, "I feel groggy…They had done something to me." Roger asked, "Do you remember anything more?" Mischief had been on the table with no clothes on, so Roger asked, "Were there people around you?" Candy and Annie are alarmed because Mischief began acting it out, taking her clothes off. The Eight Little Ones also took their clothes off.

Roger asked, "Where is Jesus in this process?" Sharon forgot about Jesus being there. Roger asked Jesus, "Why are they taking their clothes off?" I heard the words, "We are getting ready."

Roger started to pray. Roger then asked, "Is Mischief still on the table…What is happening?" I saw the Eight Little Ones holding Mischief down. Two were on each arm and leg. Butch wanted to vomit in the bucket.

Roger asked what Jesus is doing. I visualized Jesus sitting at the table trying to comfort Sharon, Annie and Candy, telling them that He is sorry for their pain. Mischief said, "But you didn't stop it!" Jesus told them He had power to stop what they did to Him, but He didn't because His suffering would end in his death and resurrection, and that salvation for humankind would come from it. They are all crying, and they asked Jesus, "Why are we naked?" Jesus told them that he had been stripped, too. He told Mischief she could come off the table, put her clothes on, and tell her story. Mischief and the Eight Little Ones all put their clothes back on.   The Eight Little Ones go back to the corner; and Mischief joins the others around the table.

Jesus told Mischief she doesn't have to act out anymore, and He would give her words to tell her story. He also told Butch that he didn't have to keep vomiting; He would give him words to express and overcome his feelings. Jesus told about the nails that they put in His hands and feet, and the spear in His body. He told them a Book was written about Him that told his story. He told them that he had to suffer first, but tremendous good would come from His suffering. There was one Bible in the room, and they were all aware that this is the book that Jesus was talking about.

Jesus got them up and took them over to the fireplace and the rocking chairs. Jesus told them that he knows the table had painful memories just like the Cross had painful memories for Him. Jesus reminded them that his death and resurrection made a public spectacle of the evil that they did to Him. Jesus told them that they would be free— but they first needed to tell their stories.

Jesus asked them if they had anything for the Surrender Box.

Candy was the first one to go to the Surrender Box. She wanted to put her mask in it.

My thoughts go to Butch throwing up in the bucket. It made me think of my daughter being held down receiving chemo injections for cancer. I remember my daughter at two, in her car seat, having to hold her white bucket in her lap as she vomited on the drive home after her chemo treatments. Mischief and Butch's pain are mine. Butch puts his bucket in the Surrender Box to give up vomiting. Mischief has a "red wig" on, takes it off and puts it in the box. Jesus asked Mischief, "What does the wig represent?" Mischief replied, "It was my covering, a kind of mask, hiding me, and I don't need it any longer." Mischief's hair is really brown.

Annie (No-Name) is left, and Jesus asks her what she wants to surrender? There are two signs in front of Annie "I am a nothing" and "I am someone with a heart." Annie takes the sign "I am nothing" and puts it in the Surrender Box. She attaches the other sign "I am someone with a heart," to her clothes.

Everyone is now sitting on the floor in a circle, and the Eight Little Ones are in the middle. Jesus is telling them they will never have to go back. They are now safe. They really don't understand what safe is yet. Jesus is telling them they are now a family, and they should help one another. He thanked them for sharing and told them to now go and play.

Roger reviewed each item that went into the Surrender Box. Today played out so differently than I expected. Jesus was focused on sharing His story with them, letting them understand His pain first. They all identified with Jesus' story. There was no more need for Mischief and the Eight Little Ones to relive their story being naked and defenseless. Butch no longer needed to vomit. It was important for Annie to have her own name and for Candy to take her mask off. Jesus drew the family closer, and they surrendered their crippling defense mechanisms which they no longer needed. Without Jesus in the room this would not have happened. Roger said, "It is all about Jesus; He is the Wonderful Counselor." Jesus called them all family.

I was done for now. They will write their book with their own stories someday.

4/9/16
Father God,

I do not know what is wrong with me. I had felt such peace this past week since my last session with Roger. But yesterday, I couldn't eat enough—"Lord, what am I doing to myself?" What am I trying to stuff/stifle/kill?

As I lay in bed, my thoughts go to my women's support group that was working through sexual abuse. Someone in our group was crying about being a little girl. I cannot connect to having been a little girl. Though dressed like one on the outside, but on inside I was empty.

Lord, what does it all mean?

Does someone need to tell me something? Is anyone hurting? Who is trying to destroy themselves? I heard, "We gave up our covering—we are scared!"

I spoke: "Where is Jesus? He is the God of all comfort. Is He in the room with you?" I hear, "He is here, He is sleeping."

You need to wake Him up and tell Him you need Him. He had fallen asleep in the boat, when the fishermen needed Him. They woke Jesus up, and He calmed the sea. He can do that for you as well.

Butch begins telling Jesus, "We need You! Jesus, we are scared! We are empty!"

Jesus responded, "It is scary to surrender what you have depended upon. It never really did what you hoped it would do, but without it you are left with nothing, and that is scary for you. Words of hope were never given you when you were little, and I want to restore those words to you."
Love, Sharon

4/14/16 1:26 AM
Father God,

I listened to a Sunday sermon on **2 Corinthians 4:8-9 We are hard pressed on every side but not crushed; perplexed but not in despair, persecuted but not abandoned, struck down but not destroyed.** I thought of the three "D" words that I often wrote about as I tried to work through my childhood abuse—damaged, destroyed, and devoured. This is a lot for a little girl to experience.

I was speaking with some women after church. One woman said that she saw fear all over me, but when she prayed, peace filled me.

Thank you Lord that Candy no longer felt alone. I identified with her not wanting to see. She understood my tears and took off her mask.

I love that No-Name took the name Annie.

Lord, you allowed me to see the connection of Mischief and Butch to the pain I endured during my daughter's cancer treatment. As Mischief had been tied down, my daughter was held down when she received her chemo. Butch vomited, and so did my daughter as we drove home after she received chemo from the oncologist.

Lord, I remember feeling responsible for my daughter's cancer. From a recurring feeling that something was really wrong with me, and I deserved to be punished. What lie am I holding on to?

Thank you Lord for guiding Mischief and the Eight Little Ones to put their clothes back on. Thank you for the way you are giving the alters words, words to tell their stories, words to heal. Thank you Jesus that you first shared your own pain with them. Thank you that they know you suffered and could identify with your pain.

Thank you that Roger said, "Where is Jesus in this process?" I was dealing with Mischief being naked on the table, neglecting to seek Jesus.

Thank you for bringing the Surrender Box and that all the alters had something to surrender. It was their pain that I felt when I crashed two days ago. I didn't know they needed to talk it out. Thank you that you gave them words for their fears: "We gave up our covering—we are scared."

Lord, why did I choose to stuff myself with food? My alters were doing a better job of surrendering their destructive behavior than I was. I need your help to understand this destructive part of me that just takes over with no sense of consequences.

Help my alters to know that you are real and that they were told lies about you. Help them to understand who deceived them, and help them to understand that I love them for all they did for me. Give them their stories.
Love, Sharon

4/26/16 Session with Roger

We discussed how I connected to Candy wearing a mask, not wanting to see the abuse. A part of me is afraid I will never get my memories, and another part doesn't want to see my memories!

Roger suggested that we go to the Conference Room, and he started to pray, asking the Lord if there was any reason why we shouldn't go there. Several different thoughts were pressing me that I knew needed to be discussed before we went anywhere.

There was my belief that I deserved my daughter's battle with cancer. I felt that I did something very bad, yet I had no idea what. I believe this was a buried lie one of my alters had carried all these years.

During my women's group, I was touched by a video series by Julie Woodley, "Wildflowers Grow in Brooklyn" and the session, "Healing Father and Mother Wounds." They discussed problems about mothers, fathers, bonding, and belonging, which I couldn't identify with at all. I was touched by the woman in the video who had a multiple personality – especially how she was comforted by another woman in the group.

Right after this interaction, the counselor in the video asked viewers to join her for the healing of their bodies. As we surrendered our bodies, I began hearing, "Wait, we are not done yet! What about what our hands have done? What about where our feet have taken us? What about what our eyes have seen? What about what we have tasted? What about what our ears have heard?" My buttons were pushed. Before I went home, the group's assistant took me in a room for individual prayer. As I started to pray, tears ran down my face, and I felt pain because of my hands from the evil they had been forced to do.

Butch was the one that said, "I am the one who overeats. I feel like a fire hydrant, under pressure, not knowing how to release all these painful feelings.

Roger prayed to Jesus to release all that has held Butch down all these years. I now visualize a fire hydrant, and I see Jesus in his robe with a large wrench opening up both sides of the hydrant. I see the water gushing out of both sides, going all over the ground. I start to chuckle, because next I see the Four Little Ones and the Eight Little

Ones playing in the water that was flooding the street. Jesus took something that was traumatic, and turned it into something fun for the alters to enjoy.

5/10/16 Session with Roger

Roger started with a prayer regarding my hands and then asked the Lord for an image or scene.

I was having a difficult time focusing. I eventually saw both Mischief and Butch sharing one chair in the Conference Room, a place in my heart. Roger asked if any alters know about the abuse regarding my hands. Mischief and Butch, hearing the question, are both troubled.

I see someone very small holding a knife in the air, but hesitated to share this with Roger and Connie? I am also hearing Mischief saying the words: "I didn't want to do this!" I start thinking about Abraham, Isaac, and the sacrifice. I heard Mischief, "Jesus, where are you?" Jesus speaks about being the Sacrifice and how He came to set us free.

Then I hear a man say, "Regarding the sacrifice, this is what you are supposed to do!"

Roger prayed and asked the Lord to give the alters peace. I next see Jesus on the floor, and both Mischief and Butch are on His lap. They are both looking at the holes in Jesus' hands. Mischief speaks of wanting a new pair of hands. Jesus replies, "No, you don't need new hands; you need to tell your story." Jesus then tells Mischief that her heart will be relieved and she will receive forgiveness.

He tells all of them about forgiveness, that if He baptizes them, their whole body will feel clean and forgiven. Jesus fills the bathtub. Jesus told them He died for them. Jesus told them that He would come and live in their hearts. Mischief and Butch say YES! They are baptized. Mischief feels better after the baptism.

Jesus, Mischief, and Butch leave the bathroom and go over to the Conference table, and there is a cake to celebrate their baptism. The other alters join around the table, and they all celebrate. Butch and Mischief are still sharing the same chair; it is as if they are attached at the hip.

I vaguely had seen a knife in the air, and it must be connected to the sacrifice. Mischief wanted to put the knife in the Surrender Box. Mischief and Butch walk to the Surrender Box. Mischief is holding the knife, but Butch takes it from her hands and puts it in the box.

Now they are telling both Annie and Candy that Jesus lives in them. They wanted that too. Jesus offers to baptize them. Annie and Candy were sorry for what they were forced to do, and they go into the bathroom so that Jesus can baptize them and they can receive the Holy Spirit.

I now find all of us in my grandparents' kitchen, including four alters and Jesus. Mischief says, "I see the bad guys coming in the back door." Mischief tries to lock the door which leads to the basement because she senses someone behind the door. Maybe it is Ken, the man who works for my grandfather.

Ken appears in the kitchen. Mischief tells him, "You are not supposed to be in the house." Ken starts washing his hands and says, "I'm getting it ready." Mischief is holding Jesus' fingers, asking Him to take the cloudiness away. I can't see Ken's face, but I remember his overalls with his name written on the pocket.

Roger then asked, "Who are you with?" There are five other people in the kitchen, including Ken. I can vaguely see an obese man who is my grandfather, a very skinny man who is my Uncle Carl, someone who has on an animal head, and another person who is my cousin Kyle with several of his fingers missing.

Roger asked if any of the faces are becoming clearer, but they were all still vague. Roger addressed the one who has the face of an animal, asking whether he is "generational," and he answered. "No. I am the undertaker." I see Mischief clinging close to Jesus.

Roger asked if everyone is still in the kitchen, and I said, "Yes."

Jesus has a Bible out reading about a table. Jesus begins telling the alters that they belong to Him and that He paid the price for their redemption. He tells them He conquered sin and death. Then Jesus starts speaking to the evil persons in the room, quoting **1 John 1:9, If we confess our sins, he is faithful and just and will forgive us our sins and purify us from all unrighteousness**. Mischief is happy that Jesus is telling this to the bad guys. The bad guys flee.

The alters are telling Jesus that they were very evil. They ask Jesus if they could go back to the Conference Room where they feel safe.

They are all back in the Conference Room and asking Jesus why He took them back to the kitchen. Jesus replied, "I want you to confront the evil in your past and its control over you." They are all sitting around the fireplace, and Jesus is asking them what happened today, and they said it was frightening.

Roger asked me if there were any loose ends. I answered that my alters have a story to tell, that is more a heart issue than a hand issue.

5/31/16 Session with Roger

I told Roger about the time, about twenty years ago, I felt an evil spirit coming from the Masonic Temple across from my grandparent's home. I had gone back there with the pastoral care minister of my church and another friend. When they began picking up pine cones in front of the Masonic Temple, I started freaking out.

I asked Roger if he can feel evil. Roger explained that he has felt evil in locations, at a house, in a basement where there was a "foundational curse," but not in people.

I told Roger about my experience of having emotions accompanied by images. Recently, during a service, I could see a cloud come down covering the people worshipping, just when my pastor said he felt the Lord's Presence. Roger said sometimes alters can see into the spirit realm. Roger talked about two different clients who both had seen a warrior angel standing in the corner of the counseling room. He said that could be the alters seeing into the spirit realm.

I told Roger that I heard cursing in my head last night and wondered it if might be Mischief being afraid in the kitchen when Ken said, "I am getting it ready."

Roger prayed for guidance and direction and asked the Lord to take Sharon and the alters to the place of greatest need for their healing. Sharon prayed for Mischief and the alters, asking the Lord to bring them healing today.

I saw Mischief and Butch sharing a chair again in the Conference Room. Jesus is there telling them that they need to go back to what happened and tell their stories to be freed of the evil. Mischief said, "I hate that house!" We are now at my grandparent's home, and Jesus enters, followed by the four alters and the Eight Little Ones. The Eight Little Ones are told to stay in the living room.

The four alters and Jesus are in the kitchen. I can see Mischief is shaking. There is a chair near the kitchen window and a yellow step stool by the stove. Jesus is telling them, "The bad guys are gone forever and you don't have to have them here to tell your story."

Mischief said, "I don't know why they did that to me!" Then Butch said, "The kitchen was where I originated, and I don't remember being any other place." Mischief said, "I remember my birthday and it was supposed to be a happy day, but it was anything but!"

Mischief remembered that they made her take her clothes off. She was really scared. They made the Eight Little Ones come into the kitchen and take their clothes off too. They tied Mischief to the table, and the Eight Little Ones had to hold the ropes.

I see Butch right there crying by the table close to Mischief. I see a paint brush, and Ken is painting Mischief with "poop." She is thinking, "This is my birthday!" Mischief asks Jesus, "Can I leave this scene now?" Jesus says, "Tell the story, I am right here." Butch reaches out to touch her hand that is tied down.

Mischief keeps saying, "Jesus, I really want to go, I want to leave here." Jesus says, "They'll never hurt you again." Mischief says "I don't want to look like poop! Why is he doing this?"

Butch is angry, "Those bastards! I can't believe they did that to you. I'd like to kick them where it hurts." Candy is sitting on the chair near the window, and she says, "I wish I had my mask on; this is too hard to watch." Candy and Annie get up and walk to the other side of the table to hold Mischief's hand. Butch gets up on the table and is lying next to Mischief. "I don't want you to be alone. We are in this together."

Mischief spoke, "The fat man is so mean; he tried to drug me so I could only see cloudy, but Jesus took away the clouds, and I know he is my grandfather." Someone said, "The fat man is a mean son of a b----." Mischief responds, "I shake in front of him all the time."

Someone says, "We're here to celebrate your birthday." Butch says, "Let's just tie the bastards up and shoot them." Mischief says, "I just want to go home." They painted my face, and I look like poop. I stink! Someone is now cutting my beautiful hair. I am aware that I am five years old, and it is my birthday. I see a small birthday cake on the counter. It is made of poop, and they want me to eat it! That's what they want me to feel like…a piece of poop. Ken fed me the cake. But they didn't count on Jesus living in me, and me knowing I am a child of God!

Jesus says, "Way to go, Sherry!" Mischief questions Jesus, "Why did you say way to go Sherry, when my name is Mischief?" Jesus said, "Sherry and you are one, just like I am one with the Father."
Mischief is talking to Jesus:

They can do what they want to my body, but they can't destroy my heart. They think I am stupid! The skinny man is getting on top of me, and I hear the words, Take that! He is hurting me. I feel the cold metal table on my back. I feel like I want to die. You know when you told me about the nails going into You. It feels like a nail is going into my body. The skinny man gets off me and I am untied and flipped over onto my stomach. I can feel the cold table. My hands are tied again. Now Ken is on top of me and putting a nail into me. I ask Jesus, 'Why didn't you stop it?' I see tears running down His face. Now I am untied and I hear my grandfather call my grandmother. She comes down to take me upstairs and put me into the tub. Tears are coming down my face, and I am aware that I am alone and helpless. I was a nothing, and no one was safe in this house. I thought my grandmother loved me, but she was one of them.

I can see Jesus standing in the bathroom. Mischief's hair is still all chopped off, but she is clean with clean clothes on. I tell Mischief to go into the living room with Jesus to find Butch, Candy, Annie, and the Eight Little Ones. Jesus begins healing her chopped off hair. He starts to comb it, and it becomes long and curly again!

We are in the living room and Jesus picks Mischief up with one arm and Butch in the other. He says, "I am so proud of you, we can go now."

Jesus gets in a car, and we are all headed to a nearby pool. Jesus says, "We need to have some fun." I see Jesus going down the slide into the pool. Jesus says, "This is where I would have brought you for your birthday. I am so sorry for what they did to you." Butch is telling Jesus, "I am sorry I used bad words." Jesus tells Butch, "You were trying to express your pain." Jesus is giving them all swimming masks to play in the water. This is a mask Candy enjoys!

There is a table set for a party with a cake and sandwiches. Five candles are on the cake. Everyone is eating, happy, and having fun.

I opened my eyes, Roger told me that everything I described is in line with Satanism. Satanism tries to twist or reverse truth from what is good to what is evil. The hardest thing to accept was that even my grandmother was untrustworthy, an enabler of their evil doings.

7/11/16 Session with Roger

I begin by telling Roger, "I feel like I'm falling apart on the inside."

On 2/20/91 the Lord guided me to read the book of Deuteronomy. This was the first time I felt the Lord had directed me to a specific Biblical book.

Reading Deuteronomy was constantly bringing me to tears. I decided to write down passages I highlighted years ago, and share them with Roger:

Deuteronomy 1:9 At that time I said to you, you are too heavy a burden for me to carry alone. I told Roger that I loved my spirit, but not my body. I had no idea why I had such thoughts. I did know that I was dealing with lies about my body.

Deuteronomy 1:29 Then I said to you, Do not be terrified of them. The Lord your God, who is going before you, will fight for you, as he did for you in Egypt, before your very eyes, and in the desert. There you saw how the Lord your God carried you as a father carries his son, all the way you went until you reached this place. I knew that the word THEM was significant, and it stood for evil people.

Deuteronomy 4:20 But as for you, the Lord took you and brought you out of the IRON-SMELTING FURNACE, out of Egypt, to be the people of his inheritance, as you now are. Somehow the furnace would eventually be connected to my painful past and my abuse.

Deuteronomy 7:5 This is what you are to do to them. Break down their altars, smash their sacred stones, cut down their Asherah poles and burn their idols in the fire. For you are a people holy to the Lord your God. The Lord your God has chosen you out of all the peoples on the face of the earth to be his people, his treasured possession.

Deuteronomy 7:22-23 The Lord your God will drive out those nations before you, LITTLE BY LITTLE. You will not be allowed to eliminate them all at once, or the wild animals will multiply around you. But the Lord your God will deliver them over to you, throwing them into great confusion until they are destroyed. This is also my process, little by little, as I uncover all that is not of God in me.

Deuteronomy 18:10 Let no one be found among you who SACRIFICES HIS SON OR DAUGHTER IN THE FIRE.

I told Roger that every time I read these Scriptures they bring more tears to my eyes.

I was getting triggered, getting more memory. I now see Mischief holding a dead baby. She is trying to breathe into the baby, trying to bring it back to life. Mischief said, "I am sorry. They forced me to do it." There are a bunch of dead babies on the floor! Mischief asked, "Jesus, where are you?" I can see Jesus close by Mischief's side, and I see Butch sitting next to Mischief.

Someone told Mischief that she is wicked, and she believes it. Mischief said, "I hate my hands! I hate my eyes! I hate everything about me!" Butch answered, "I love you, Mischief." Mischief responded, "I hate my body; I wish I was dead!" Butch said, "It was them or us." Mischief replied, "I have blood all over my hands. This is too painful, I want to die."

Wow! I had been thinking about my struggles with food from an early age. I had a sudden thought about Candy's name, that it reminded me of the candy I used to eat when I lived at my grandparent's home, which was the beginning of my eating addiction.

I felt the pain of what Mischief carried by being forced to take innocent lives. Roger asked how old I was then. I said, "I was five. I was small. Not far from being a baby myself." Roger told me I was forced to do it, but you still have to deal with and overcome the emotional effects.

Mischief is trying to love the little dead babies. She is devastated, saying, "I don't like anything about me." Maybe that is when I started just existing, becoming empty inside.

When I was about seven, there was a fire in my house. My mother and I were home alone. I remember telling the firemen that they needed to save all my dolls (my babies). I cared about them. I didn't want them to burn up. The memory of the childhood fire triggered a horrific memory regarding a furnace.

I could see the abusers threw the dead babies into the furnace fire. They didn't want a trace of evidence, all would be gone. So that is why the Lord directed me to **Deuteronomy 4:20 about the "iron-smelting furnace."** I knew years ago that this Scripture held some significance for me.

So now all the dead babies are gone, but I am left with this big hole inside of me and don't know what to do with it.

April 1991 – Twenty-eight years ago I was at a Prophetic Healing Conference hosted by my church.

During the Conference, hosted by Doris and her team, I stood up for the breaking of vows, the breaking of generational ties, and the breaking of documents, relating to the paperwork at the Clinic in Texas, my birth certificate, and other documents. I went forward for prayer, and I just laid on the floor.

- *Doris said, "You have no fear."*
- *Doris asked, "What happened 12 years ago?" I told her I went back to church.*

Doris's prayer started:

- *"What do you need to surrender?"*
- *I said, "Blood." Jim prayed for cleansing of my blood.*
- *Doris asked, "What else do you need to surrender?"*
- *I said "Dead babies."*
- *"How many?"*
- *I said, "Dead babies."*
- *"Where are the babies?"*
- *I said, "Dead."*
- *Doris asked a second time, "How many?"*
- *I said, "So many."*
- *I am numb and I cannot feel, and Doris prays for a new heart.*
- *Inside I hear the words, "death threats."*
- *Doris asks, "What do you need to burn?"*
- *I said, "Journals, dreams, books, tapes, and pictures." I recall the verses in Deuteronomy that say "Burn their idols in the fire." I remember thinking years ago, these are the only proofs I have of the reality of the abuse and my sanity in attesting to what happened.*

After the church conference (Doris and her team and several members from my church) came to my home and had me get two garbage bags, and fill them with the things I needed to surrender, and Doris took them home with her to be burned in a fire.

The Lord was telling me to stop striving, fighting, and rest in Him.

Roger asked me to visualize Mischief, and then asked, "Mischief, do you have memory today of seeing Jesus?" Mischief replied, "Jesus was next to me on one side and Butch on the other." Roger asked, "What was your take on Jesus?" Mischief replied, "The emptiness and the anxiety still take over me."

Roger asked, "Lord, before we go any further, is there anything you want to share with us?"

Jesus said, "The babies are alive and happy in heaven." Jesus told Mischief, "They killed my body, but I rose and the babies have risen, and I want to heal you." Before, I saw Mischief holding the dead babies; now I see Jesus with Mischief and Butch on His lap.

- Jesus told both Mischief and Butch, "I died to set you free."
- Jesus said, "I know your hearts were broken, falling like Humpty Dumpty, but I will create new hearts in both of you."
- Mischief asked about her bloody hands. Jesus replied, "I will make them whiter than snow."
- Jesus said, "When I baptized you, you became clean."
- Jesus reminded them, "I am always living inside of you."

Butch said, "Let's get out of here!" Mischief went out with Butch to play.

Roger asked me, "What are your thoughts?" I said, "They defiled my body and that is certainly the reason why I hated my body so much." Mischief believed that she is wicked. She hated her hands and eyes.

Roger asked me what I learned today. I said, "I made some connections with what surfaced from the alters."

I shared with Roger another Scripture in Deuteronomy, which the Lord had recently led me, which related to the "Eight Little Ones."

Deuteronomy 1:39 And THE LITTLE ONES that you said would be taken captive, your children who do not yet know good from bad—they will enter the land. I will give it to them, and they will take possession of it.

Roger asked, "Before we go further, is anyone interested in integrating today? I told the alters, it would be like the beautiful finished picture of a jigsaw puzzle: "You did what Sharon needed you to do. You were a blessing to Sharon. Now Sharon is older, and it would make her soul so much stronger if you would now INTEGRATE. It is up to you."

Butch said, "I want in." Mischief said, "You are not going without me!" Candy and Annie are happy to go. The Eight Little Ones are going to follow their leader, Mischief. They form a circle around Sharon and hold hands. Roger said, "We want to thank you for all that you have done for Sharon. Now walk towards the center of the circle, towards Sharon, and go ahead in." They are finally all inside.

Roger prayed for the alters and thanked the Lord. Sharon said, "They are trying to figure out where they want to hang out inside my body"

- Jesus said, "Your body is the temple of the Holy Spirit".

- Jesus said, "You have to stop believing the lies. I have shown you truth. Walk in it."
- Jesus said, "You are free."
- Jesus said, "I will complete what I started."
- Jesus told me he loves me.
- Satan only has power if I give it to him.

Chapter Five

ANDREW, BEN, FLO (Afraid), VIOLET (Fear)

Session with Roger 7/26/16

I wanted to talk with Roger about a dead cat, which came to mind when I was reading over my notes from the last session. I wondered if the dead cat was somehow related to the dead babies that came up two weeks ago.

The Lord had revealed to me deep feelings when I was begging the firemen to save my dolls (my babies) from the fire in my home when I was a child.

Roger started in prayer. As I try to focus, Jesus and Sharon are heading to the Conference Room.

Then my vision of the scene changes, and I find that I am now a child on the boardwalk behind my home. I can see the dead cat. I picked it up and asked Jesus, "Did I kill this cat too?" I was crying. Jesus was there with a shovel making a grave for the cat. Jesus buried the dead cat, and on top of the grave He put a tiny cross. I told Jesus, "I am sorry, I don't know what I did." I was feeling a lot of emotion. I talked about a vague memory of getting a dead animal for my birthday.

Jesus and Sharon are now back in the Conference Room. We open the second door, and a mist is blocking my view. Jesus tells me to walk through the mist. I see someone playing with a truck. He speaks, "I pretend I'm little, but I'm really big." This is Andrew who is seven. He said, "I am afraid of Butch, and I killed the cat behind the garage. My grandfather, Uncle Carl, and Ken made me do it." Jesus said, "The bad guys can't hurt you any longer. You were forced to do it!" Andrew said, "I'm sorry, it wasn't in my heart to kill an animal."

Jesus takes Andrew to the brook at the bottom of my grandfather's property. After Jesus baptizes Andrew He tells him, "I now live inside of you." Jesus had washed his sins away. Andrew, continued, "That is all I did, and now I want to be with the others."

Jesus, Sharon, and Andrew are back in the Conference Room. Andrew said, "There are more in the dungeon." Andrew continued, "I can take you to the dungeon, but I'm not going in. They are trapped down there; you'll have to get them out." I let Jesus go first. I see bars and gates just like the verses in Deuteronomy. Jesus opens the gate and walks right in. Someone is hiding in the dark. Jesus invites them to come out and says, "I came to help you." Sharon encourages three alters to come out. There is one boy and two girls; all looking filthy. They said, "We are the scum of the earth." Jesus introduces Himself and Sharon. Jesus then says, "Come, follow me." The alters walk up the stairs. They only had known darkness and are blinded by the light. They are dressed in black coverings. Sharon named them Darkness One, Darkness Two, and Darkness Three.

Jesus takes the boy and two girl alters to the brook to clean them up. They don't know anything about water, people, or having fun. Sharon and Andrew are trying to make them feel comfortable. Sharon and Andrew are splashing, but the others don't join in because they are afraid of the water. Jesus has them sit on rocks in the water. Andrew tries to comfort the new alters. He said, "I'm sorry you are afraid. I was afraid too; they made me kill a cat." One alter has some fingers missing. I immediately think of my cousin Kyle who had several of his fingers missing. I also think about my cousin who was with the three men when I was raped in the kitchen. The alter said, "He took off my finger, so I took off his finger." I said, "Did they make me take off my cousin's finger too?" Roger reminded me I was forced to do evil things. I started crying and I asked, "How do you let go of what you did?" Roger asks, "Are you asking me or Jesus?" I asked Jesus, "How do you let go of such guilty memories?" Jesus said,

- What they meant for evil, I will make for good.
- You are sealed by My blood and nothing can get in.
- You are not what you've done, but what I've done for you.
- I took your sin away on the Cross.
- Your heart, not your hands, represent who you are.

I felt such a strong need to pray for my cousin what was on my heart. I prayed for Kyle and all that he went through, for all the evil done to him. I prayed that he would find answers, resolution, and freedom in Christ.

We are down at the brook with the three alters, Darkness One, Darkness Two, and Darkness Three. Their dark coverings were then removed. I asked Jesus if he would restore Darkness One's finger. Jesus calls the alter Ben (Darkness One) and heals his finger. Jesus goes to Afraid (Darkness Two) and asks, "I want you to surrender your name Afraid." She responds, "The brook is flowing so just call me Flo." Jesus then goes to Fear (Darkness Three) and asks, "What can we call you?" She sees violets by the brook so she says, "Call me Violet."

Jesus asks, "Do you want to leave? We can go back to the Conference Room." Andrew, Jesus, and Sharon are there sitting on the rocking chairs. The alters never experienced chairs. Ben goes over and sits next to Andrew. The two girls are huddled in a corner of the room.

10/22/16
Father God,

It was so hard sitting down with my notes. It is hard to believe this is about me, my life. So much was robbed from me, so much was taken away: innocence, laughter, playfulness, imagination, joy, bonding, belonging, identity. Everything was corrupted by evil and lies at such a young age. Secured by demons and lies, and etched into my being.

Lord, what makes people do this? Do this to their very own family? Do this to little children?

Lord, normal feelings were robbed from me. I walk around feeling empty, nothing more than an empty shell.

They tried to destroy me completely. They inflicted on my body their shame and guilt. My abusers filled me with their lies and evil desires. The alters lived in darkness, unable to get free, bound by demons and strongholds.

They destroyed my fifth birthday. They gave me a birthday cake made of poop and forced me to eat it. Then they painted me with what was left to try to destroy me even more. They tried to destroy my hands by having them do their evil deeds. They forced me to hear things a little girl should never hear. They forced me to embrace their evil to control me. I was literally forced to eat and taste evil. I was forced to kill and destroy. Lord, how did this little girl survive such evil?

Why did Ben, Flo, and Violet say, "We are the scum of the earth." What happened to them to believe that lie? What were they forced to do?

Thank you that my alter Andrew was able to talk about killing the cat. Thank you for forgiving him and baptizing him in the brook. Thank you for healing Ben's severed finger. I pray that you would bring healing to the alters who I named Darkness One, Darkness Two, and Darkness Three. Thank you for changing their names. Thank you for telling them in the dungeon, "Come, follow me!" Lord bring life to them; restore and heal their pain. Transform them!

I know Andrew is ready to integrate, but the others are still stuck. They only have new names. They have not told their stories. Lord, why were they behind the bars and gates in the dungeon? Please restore all that was taken from them.

Love, Sharon

10/23/16
Dear Andrew, Ben, Flo, and Violet,

My name is Sherry. I was the little girl you alters protected. I was five years old. I am Sharon's inner child and I am part of Sharon, too. Sharon is almost 70. She is getting all of us help.

Jesus brought you out of the dungeon. Jesus is God, and He will help and heal us and make us whole. He will help you tell your story. They put big nails into his body to kill him. He understands. He is our Father God, our Daddy who loves us so much. The Father and His Son Jesus love you, and they will help us through the Holy Spirit.

Andrew, I am sorry that Bop, Uncle Carl, and Ken forced you to kill a cat. Jesus buried the cat and put a little cross on its grave. Your words were, "I'm sorry, it wasn't in my heart to kill an animal." Jesus forgave you and baptized you in the brook. Jesus now lives in you. We need to tell the others about Jesus. Thank you, Andrew, for caring for the others and taking us to the dungeon. Why are you afraid of Butch?

Ben, I am sorry you lost your finger. You said, "My cousin Kyle took off my finger, so you took off his finger." They made you do it. They made Andrew kill a cat. Jesus healed your finger. He wants to heal all of us. You will learn to love Jesus, and He will come to live inside your heart.

Flo and Violet, I know your names were Afraid and Fear. Thank you for letting Jesus give you new names. He will make everything new.

I am so sorry that you lived filthy in a dungeon all those years. Jesus took you to the brook to make you clean. I know you are still afraid.

I like your new names. Flo, yours came from a brook, and Violet, yours came from the flowers by the brook.

We need to hear your stories to free you. Why were you hiding? You both said, "We are the scum of the earth. Please tell us what they made you do."

Sherry said, "They raped me and put poop all over me. They made me eat poop. They made Andrew kill a cat."

Jesus will help us. What else happened when they locked you in a dungeon behind bars and gates? You will never have to go back there. I want to help you.

Love, Sherry

Session with Roger 10/25/16

I discussed with Roger the triggers from my childhood trauma that came up since my shoulder surgery. My alter Andrew was ready to integrate. Although the other alters had healings -- Ben had his finger restored, and Flo and Violet had their names changed. They still felt afraid, filthy and like the scum of the earth.

We also discussed Sherry's letter. Roger felt Sherry, the inner child, shared executive control with Sharon.

I felt grateful that I survived. I felt sad the alters had to carry my pain all these years. I felt sad they lived behind bars, gates, and were guarded by the demonic realm.

After Roger prayed, I visualized myself in the Conference Room, and I see Flo and Violet huddled in a corner.

Jesus, Sharon, Andrew, and Ben are sitting on the rocking chairs. Sharon asked Ben a question about his feelings toward Jesus. Ben replied, "Evil was done to Jesus." Ben then said, "Jesus is very loving; He restored my finger." Jesus reminds Ben, "You are not what they forced you to do, but what I have done for you."

Andrew asks Ben, "Are you ready to accept Jesus?" Ben thanks Jesus for healing his finger and then expresses sorrow for all he did. Jesus baptizes Ben in the bathtub.

Sharon is in the corner talking to the two girls. Someone said, "It is meaningless to be clean when you feel like scum. They peed and pooped all over me, I was like their toilet." Bop, my grandfather, called us scum.

Sharon asked, "Flo and Violet, what happened behind the bars and gates?" Jesus was sitting on the floor near the girls, and He was showing them how nails were put through His hands and feet. Flo said, "They stuck things in my mouth and made me choke. They stuck things in my hiney."

Flo and Violet were sitting on Sharon's lap next to Jesus. Sharon asks, "What does the word "scum" mean?" Someone responded, "Real, real, bad! This house (my grandparent's house) is a joke. They had a sandbox and a swing in the backyard liked they cared, but they did bad things to us."

Jesus gives a bottle of sweet perfume to the girls and they dab it on. Jesus ironically called it their toilet water! Jesus spoke, "I am God, and I told my disciples to 'Come follow me,' and I am telling you, 'Come follow me.'"

There is the Surrender Box in the corner. Both Flo and Violet have a picture of a toilet bowl which they put in the Surrender Box.

The alters are consumed with hatred, so Jesus tells them, "Vengeance is mine, and I will hold them accountable for what they did to you. If you keep hating you will be forever stuck." Someone asks, "What are we to do with the hate?" Jesus asks Flo, "What does hate look like to you?" Flo replied, "I want to stab him with a knife, and I want to pee and poop all over him. I want him to feel like scum."

Violet wants to surrender the hate. She drew the word "HATE" on paper in big letters and put it in the Surrender Box. Violet went over to the others.

Flo is having a hard time surrendering her hate. Jesus takes Flo out to the pond to see a trapped duck. Jesus is telling Flo, "You have two choices. You can stay stuck, or you can get free by letting go of the hate." Jesus said to the duck, "Be free!" The duck broke loose and swam away. There was power in Jesus' words and Flo saw that power.

Flo is back in the Conference Room and she writes, "Be free and let go of hatred." She puts the paper with the words into the Surrender Box.

Jesus talks to Flo and Violet about being baptized, and they go into the bathroom. First, Jesus lets them play in a bubble bath; then he changes the water and baptizes them. Jesus tells Flo that her heart will be brand new and that she will never feel like scum again.

They are all back in the Conference Room and sitting on the rocking chairs.

Jesus takes them outside to the meadow, down to a different brook, and unlike before, all the alters are now healed and playing in the water. Andrew is sitting on a rock and down from the meadow comes a cat which sits on Andrew's lap. They all are giving testimony of what Jesus did for them. Jesus asks them if they are ready to integrate back into Sharon's heart and make her so much stronger. Then Sharon can go back and get the other alters who are not free.

Andrew is the first to INTEGRATE, then comes Ben, Flo and Violet. They are all one with Sharon.

Sharon tells Sherry she doesn't have to go back in the cage, that she is a pretty little girl, and that Jesus came to set her free. Sherry replies, "Bop is a mean son-of-a-bitch and hits me all the time with the cane when it is not around my neck."

Sharon asks, "How are you able to do school?" Sherry: "In my head is a cage, and I put all the bad things there and lock it all up. Then I pretend I am a little girl." Sherry is sitting on Sharon's lap and Sharon asks her, "What is in the cage that is inside your head?" Sherry responses:

- The big black dog that is always with them
- My grandfather wanted me to lick him - I hate it
- The dog is licking me, as they are holding me down
- Bop keeps hitting me with his cane

Jesus, Sharon, and Sherry are now outside near the driveway. Sherry says, "The cage goes with me wherever I go; I can't get rid of it. The nights are really bad for me. I try to go to Nana's room so they can't get me. I don't know why my mother left me here. I live with a bunch of animals. They try to do anything to kill everything in me."

Jesus, Sharon and Sherry are going to the cottage.

11/19/16 at 5:40 AM
Dear Roger,

Things are getting worse on my end. I am so restless. The night before last, I managed only three hours, and that is how it has been these past few weeks. I just can't stand living inside this body.

Last night, before going back to bed, I had prayed through the two-page spiritual warfare prayer that you gave me. When I got into bed, I felt antsy all over. I went to bed at 10 p.m. and laid there sleepless for two hours. I was up from 12 to 2 a.m. trying to write and pray. I listened to Derek Prince. Praise music wasn't helping either. I am exhausted but can't sleep.

I am getting worse, not better. How can this situation benefit the healing of my shoulder surgery? Why am I being tortured? Why am I being broken?

In Christ, Sharon

11/19/16
Dear Lord,

I sent out an S.O.S. e-mail to Roger. I am at my wit's end. Lord, I feel like I might have a breakdown.

I hate my body even more.

Your Word tells me to cast my cares upon You. So I am casting them onto You. I need sleep; my surgery needs healing.

Lord, your Holy Spirit dwells in my body. I need to realize You are purging out the trauma to free me, but I need help to withstand the process.

Lord, I know You love me. I know You are healing me. Speak, for Your servant is listening.
Love, Sharon

Father God's Reply
Dear Sharon,

Jesus knows this process is hard, but always remember His words, "I go before you, and I am within you."

You are in the fire, but like in Daniel and the fiery furnace, the only things that burned were the ropes that bound him.

They have no power, I have the victory. I have a purpose and a plan.

The pieces are coming together. What has bound you all these years is surfacing. The evil deeds will be exposed and healed. The pieces are coming together.

Your treasure will be found in the darkness when I bring light, and I will disable all that was done to destroy you. I will repay you for what the locust has eaten. I will open the door for you to do a new ministry.

You will be strengthened. Never doubt my goodness.

Sharon, you and Sherry are strong. I will heal both of you.

Hope, believe, trust, and surrender to all that I lay before you. I will give you memory, and I will give you words. I am making you complete and nothing will stop you.

Abide in me, even in the hard times and places. You are precious to me.
Love, Your Daddy and Lord

Session with Roger 11/22/16

I told Roger I was hardly feeling myself on Saturday when I sent my cry for help. Roger inquired again if I was sharing control with someone. I told him I felt tormented, and maybe someone was trying to break my will. I couldn't get peaceful, couldn't sleep, and when I journaled I could only cry.

My pastor was giving a message on, "Your Treasure in Heaven." At the end of the service he called on several people to stand up, telling them they were a treasure. I was one, and my pastor declared,

"Sharon, you are a treasure. I break the power of the enemy over you. Every curse that was spoken over you has been broken this morning. The light shines in the darkness. God will shine His light on you. The hope that you have will not be lost, because the Enemy has been served notice in your life and now is threatening more than ever. You see the Enemy wants to destroy you Sharon, because he feels he paid a price for you. He had no right to you. From the beginning says the Lord, For you are mine says God."

Roger talked about how we were not finished with Sherry and the graveyard. He began talking again about "executive control." He explained that I share mixed feelings with someone within.

I replied, "Feelings of torment and torture were new extreme feelings for me. I sensed that they were trying to break me down."

Roger said your alters can even make you amnesic. Alters can decide if they want a person to hear or not.

Roger prayed and then I prayed for Sherry. I hear, "I am now inside a box." Roger asked if it was dark, and Sherry said, "Yes."

Lord, please remove Sherry from the box and bring her into the light in Jesus' name. The abusers put things inside the box that crawl all over Sherry including a snake and spiders. Sherry said, "They tell me I am evil and leave me in there a long time. They said I would stay there until I learn my lesson that I am a dog."

I am somewhere in the cemetery; I am in a mausoleum. It is so dark, and they have drugged me. I wrote something long time ago about "whom I belong to." Sherry is holding on to Jesus' finger saying, "You're God."

I can visualize my grandfather driving his black car by the mausoleum where the box was located. I will hurry up and get inside the box, or I will be in big trouble. I am back inside the box, but Jesus is hiding in the corner nearby. My grandfather comes in, opens the box, and asks if I learned my lesson. I asked him what the lesson was. My grandfather said, "You are evil, and you are a dog." I hate him. He told me to go back into the box, and then he put this real big spider in the box to crawl all over me. I was frightened out of my mind.

My grandfather left, and Jesus opened the box letting me out. Jesus opened the barred door and we went back to the cottage. I told Jesus, "I will never be free." Jesus said it remains in my head: the box, the cage, the dog, and the cane. I replied, "I have so much in my head." Jesus asked, "Who took you out of the cage and the box?" Sherry said, "You did." Jesus told Sherry He was trying to free her.

Sherry said, "I hate him, I hate what he did to my body, and I hate my body." Jesus replied, "Sherry, but now I live in your body." Sherry said, "Then I won't hate my body, but will I hate what he did to me." Sherry is resisting Jesus. Jesus is trying to get Sherry to understand what self-hatred and hateful thoughts about her grandfather do. Jesus said, "I can't live inside someone who lives in their hate."

Jesus asked Sherry, "Do you know I love you? Do you trust Me? Take your grandfather and put him into My hands. Put the hate into My hands and leave it there." Sherry said, "I will do it because I don't want You to leave me." Then Jesus said, "Take the cage, the dog, the cane, and the box that is in your head and put it into my hands, give them to me." Sherry said, "How do I do that?" Jesus said, 'Say I surrender it.' Sherry said, "Okay, I surrender it." Now Jesus declares, "Be Free!" Sherry reported that the images immediately left her head. Jesus asked Sherry how she felt, and she replied "I am free."

Roger said Sherry (the inner child) was sharing executive control with Sharon this weekend. The disturbing memories were causing the lost sleep. Roger said the dog, cage, cane were typical items of ritual abuse.

Roger said Sherry had to surrender the hate to get the overwhelming images out of her head. I told Sherry we had more people we needed to try to free and I needed her help. She said okay.

Roger said, "Interesting how it works with our Wonderful Counselor. It takes only an hour for Him, and He changes things."

Session with Roger 1/3/17

It had been almost a month since our last visit. I took most of December off to enjoy my family and my 70th birthday. The Lord had overridden the trauma of my horrific childhood birthday of many years ago. I had a wonderful 70th with family and friends.

Roger said, "What do we deal with today?" I said, "I brought bullet points of what I discussed with the Lord in prayer.

"First, let's ask the Lord where He wants to take us today." Roger prays for direction. I started praying as well.

I see myself as a little child sitting on the floor in a Christian psychologist's office. I have an inability to put into words my tears. I am angry because no one can hear my pain...I feel sad...I picked the Godliest counselors I could find, and I just receive more pain and rejection.

I now see Jesus sitting on the psychologist's floor with me. I try asking the little girl what her name is and I get no answer - she is not talking. The little girl is questioning Jesus,

- Where were You when I needed You?
- They told me You wouldn't come and help me
- I was a pretty little girl and they destroyed me
- They took my beauty away

Jesus addresses her as Sherry. Jesus is trying to tell Sherry what they did to Him, that they crucified Him. With tears, Sherry said:

- You were destroyed as an adult; I was destroyed as a child
- I had no happy, no funny, and no silly
- You had a family that loved you

Jesus thanked Sherry for acting out her pain. Sherry wanted to know why so many people in her life couldn't hear her pain. Jesus replied, "They couldn't understand the depth of your pain, but I know completely what you went through. Nothing is hidden from Me."

Sherry told Jesus, "Thank you for coming today. That day many years ago was a real painful day for me. Thank you for fixing and restoring my brokenness from it."

Jesus said, "Thank you for forgiving the psychologist for being unable to help you."

Now Roger asks, "How did you feel about the experience you just had with Sherry? I said, "I feel it was an agonizing day, but Jesus healed that day for me with what He showed and said to me."

Roger tells me to keep seeking the Lord and let Him reveal the next step. Don't try to figure everything out by yourself.

Chapter Seven

BETSY

1/7/17
Dear Lord,

I woke up and again my back was so painful. I am just sitting here with my thoughts about my conversation with a friend last night. Her question was, "What if your body never changes?" I am in tears at the thought of having to accept that.

I told my friend, "Then, they have won." I am almost 70, and I have no control over the despair I feel about my body.

Thank you for my friend's question. Thank you for the pain I need to confront and resolve. I can't even imagine what freedom from my negativity would feel like.

Thank you Lord that all they did to my body didn't destroy me. Thank you for protecting my spirit. Thank you for the faith that saw me through. Thank you for enabling me to see and hear You.

Lord, I am sorry for the pain of the Cross and all You endured to set the captives free.

I trust You that someday I will not only survive, but thrive. I trust You will deliver and transform me.

Lord, help me with my health and the food I take into my body.

Help my back and shoulder to heal.

Thank you for the energy that is returning to me.

I seek Your peace that passes all understanding. Help me to move closer to Your heart and to trust all that I know about Your love,

mercy, healing power, and your faithfulness to "do immeasurable more than I ask or think."
Love, Sharon

Two hours later. . . . .

"Who is this alter inside that is feeling pain? Can you tell me your name? Is it your body that is hurting? Who feels 'they have won?' Why do you feel that? Who shared with my pastor those exact words, 'They have won?'" I love you little one. Thank you for your tears.

"Are you the one who looks at other children with envy? Are you jealous as you look at others with their healthy bodies?"

Lord Jesus, I pray You will help this little one process the source of our anguish.

Images start coming:

I see two small children sitting on the floor. They are the same size. Sherry's arm is around Betsy, who is five. Jesus is just watching these two interact. Betsy is saying:

- I am nothing and a nobody
- I am garbage
- I am disgusting to look at
- They taught me how to kill
- I am afraid they will kill me too
- I know how to use the axe
- I can chop a tail off a cat and a head off a dog
- I don't feel, the evil has made me numb

Sherry said, "The abusers are gone forever, Jesus can help us. Sherry is crying for Betsy's pain. "I am so sorry. You are a little girl like me."

- I am under their control
- They tell me to chop and I chop
- I don't think about it, I just do as I am told
- That is how I lost my beautiful hair, they told someone to chop
- I didn't want to lose anything else so I chop
- My hands are not connected to my heart
- I have an empty body; I am only a shell inside

- I do bad things. I am garbage, so being in a garbage bag isn't hard for me. It is where I belong, and, at least, I am covered.

"You are not garbage!" Sherry said. "They made you kill and destroy and that stopped you from feeling. They didn't give you a choice. Betsy, you are a beautiful girl, even though your hair is chopped off. Jesus can restore your hair and give you a new heart for your body. Would you like that?

I see Sherry on the floor sitting on Jesus' lap. She is encouraging Betsy to join her. Jesus touches Betsy's hair, and she feels her hair growing back. She can now feel a new heart as well. Betsy's body is being restored. I see new veins, muscles, organs being restored in Betsy's body. Betsy and Sherry start to play ring-a-round the rosie.

We will tell Roger all that you shared. You will be able to feel because you have a new heart.

Isaiah 52:14 Just as there were many who were appalled at him— his appearance was so disfigured beyond that of any man and his form marred beyond human likeness.

Betsy, those words point to what was done to both you, me, and Jesus. His outsides were disfigured, and our inside was destroyed.

1/31/17

It's 3 a.m. and I cannot sleep, my left leg is antsy. I had been dealing with what is called "dog programming."

An Experience with the Holy Spirit at the Altar of my Church:

As I stood at the altar, I could feel and see a hand on my left shoulder. I sensed this question, "What do you want?" I said, "A mantel like Moses to deliver my people who are in bondage." Then I saw this mantel being put on my shoulder and it was blue. I was wondering if this was just my imagination. I kept thinking, "Hand of God." I could sense someone behind me. Then I could see someone taking off a dog leash chained around my neck. I heard the words, "You are not a dog, you are My child." The experience ended.

Session with Roger on 1/31/17

I really went astray when you were unable to see me last week. I ate food containing sugar and flour and then threw it up. I wound up disgusted with myself and unable to work on my childhood trauma.

When I shared at cell group, I received prayer which was very positive. I had been feeling so alone. After the prayer I could tell I felt different, and by the next day I was out of my depression.

But there remained much inside unconnected.

I felt like Sherry paved the way for Betsy. Betsy said, "I am like garbage; I chopped the tail off a cat and head off a dog; they told me to chop and I did." There is nothing inside Betsy and there is emptiness inside of me. Roger reminded me that Jesus said, "You are not garbage."

Roger asked, "Where are we going today?" Then we started in prayer. I prayed for the restoring of Betsy and whatever was unconnected. Roger prayed, "Lord Jesus, guide Sharon in her thought process."

Sharon said, "I can see Jesus, Sherry and Betsy on the floor. Betsy is looking at the things on the floor which I had brought to my therapist's office. The axe is lying on the floor. Betsy is making a black square with a crayon: it is the altar in the graveyard, which you can see from my grandparent's house.

Betsy had a white dress on. She started out pretty. They are surrounding the grave, but I can't see who they are; little animals are on the ground. She put a circle around the black square, because people surround her in a circle.

I know that Ken is there. I cannot see his face, but I see his dog standing next to him. I feel like someone is taking my pretty white dress off. Possibly, it is Nana. I don't know why I am the only one inside the circle that is naked.

I see lights from lanterns high on poles, and I hear them singing. I am crying. I am trying to get Nana to put my dress back on, but she walks away from me. The one person I thought loved me is gone.

They are all yelling, "You are a dog." I am crying and thinking, "No, I am a little girl." I see my grandfather; he's in the circle too. He tells me, "You are nothing but a dirty dog, and when I tell you to move, you move!" I keep saying, "I want my Nana."

Betsy is up on the altar being tied down. Sherry is holding her hand, and Jesus is there too. Jesus is telling Betsy, "You don't have to actually go through the pain again, just allow yourself to tell the story. I am here with you.

March 2002
"PIGS"

The image was clear. I could see this mini-bus (possibly school bus) filled with "PIGS."

Suddenly, I feel like a bright light is illuminating everything. I can only see bodies, heads are gone, even my grandfather is unclear. My grandfather is obese; I know it is him. He has a black robe on. Bop says to me, "You are evil, a dog, nothing but s----." Ken is there, I can't see his face, but I know his outline. People are in dark clothes. Someone is putting a mask over my face. Maybe they are giving me some kind of drug.

I am laid down, and I can't see people. I feel the cold stone on my back. Even though I can't see, I can hear. Betsy is numb.

My grandfather is at my feet. He keeps telling me I am evil. He is going to put a snake in my body because I am evil. I can feel something going inside of me. Someone is now on top of me, I don't know if it is a dog or a person dressed as a dog. Then something is in my mouth. My grandfather says, "Take that." I can hardly breathe. I feel like something is put all over me. My face is being licked and even my privates. I don't know if it is a dog or a person. Someone is in the circle on two feet, skinny like my Uncle Carl. I think he is dressed like a dog. He's barking to confuse me. I hear the words, "You belong to Satan." He is putting something in my privates that feels like a knife, and he is saying, "Take that, you evil one."

Betsy is saying to Jesus, "I feel numb. They untie me and flip me over like a pancake and tie me again. My grandfather is putting a snake in my hiney." My grandfather says, "You will slither like a snake all the days of your life." My uncle is now on top of me, and I feel the knife is cutting me open. He is saying, "You will bark like a dog." Jesus unties Betsy, and she come down off the altar.

****

Sherry and Betsy walked down to the brook with Jesus and entered the water, trying to be careful of the stones. Betsy said, "My whole body is disgusting." Jesus showed both Betsy and Sherry the holes in His hands and feet.

Betsy said, "I need my body healed." Jesus said, "I can baptize you, and your whole body will be well. I will restore your hair. You will be able to release your emotions and confess your sins." Betsy asked, "What are sins?" Jesus replied, "Bad choices." Betsy said, "I hate those people who made me feel like s----." Jesus told her how he was treated, how He had to forgive to be free." Jesus asked Betsy to surrender the people who hurt her. Betsy said she didn't understand, but would do it.

Jesus baptized her, and she was beaming as she came out of the water. Jesus said, "I am sorry for all that you went through Betsy, but you are now free."

Betsy and Sherry then both put on small dresses and shoes.

Roger said, "So Betsy and Sherry are completely healed from all of that." I commented, "The hardest part was seeing my grandmother walk away." Roger said, "You didn't expect her to abandon you." I replied, "When Nana went away, I didn't have anyone." Roger said, "In the end you found out you had Jesus." Sharon commented, "Jesus made them disappear like magic." Roger responded, "Jesus said He wanted you to remember, so you can get beyond the hurt." Betsy's body was restored.

Roger said, "Jesus had asked Betsy to confess her sins to have her body healed. Betsy also had to surrender her abusers to Jesus." What you described is ritual abuse. We live in a fallen world, and Jesus came to seek and save those who are lost. Roger closed in prayer. I prayed

thanking the Lord that Betsy was no longer alone. I thanked the Lord
for last night and that he took the dog chain off my neck.

Chapter Eight

VALENTINE'S DAY

2/14/17 Session with Roger

I asked Roger how common it was with childhood abuse to be numb, not to feel as an adult. He said, "It is not unusual."

I told Roger about a speaker at an Aglow meeting who, after concluding, requested those who needed prayer to come to the altar. Tearfully, I knelt and visualized a small white dress laying on the altar. It was the dress that I wore at the ritual ceremony when I was abused. I felt immediately that I needed to forgive my grandmother for her involvement in my devastating childhood abuse. I was comforted when a gentle man came up behind me to pray with me.

Roger asked, "You had a peaceful week?" I responded, "Yes, and when I feel this peaceful, it seems like there really is nothing wrong with me.

Roger and I both prayed to the Wonderful Counselor. I needed to surrender my impatience. I had expected so much in my last session with the image I got at the altar. I said, "I give up my will to You, Lord."

I sat quietly, and I saw in my spirit I am at the bottom of a brook with Jesus, Betsy, and Sharon. Betsy is asking the question, "How do you love your body after what you have gone through?" Sharon pipes in, "You are not what they did to you; you are what Jesus did for you."

Betsy replies, "This life is all I've known." Betsy tells Jesus, "I know you gave me a new heart, but I still feel hollow inside." Jesus responds, "Everyone has emptiness, but the holes can be filled by the

Holy Spirit." Betsy asks, "What does Holy Spirit mean?" Jesus makes a hole in the ground and then takes some water from the brook and fills the hole. Jesus says, "This is how the Holy Spirit will fill you." Betsy said, "I got it."

Sharon asked Betsy if she had any more trauma to share.

Jesus began telling Betsy she was originally part of Sharon's heart and broke off to sacrifice herself and shield Sharon from the trauma. Jesus asked if she wanted to integrate and be a healthy part of the heart instead of being by herself. Betsy approved.

Jesus was showing Betsy her part of Sharon's heart with a puzzle piece that fitted into the heart's bottom left hand corner. Jesus offered to walk Betsy inside the heart. They walk inside, Betsy puts the puzzle piece in place, and now she is INTEGRATED. Only a small part of the heart was still missing, at the bottom of the heart where it comes to a point.

Roger prayed, thanking Jesus for being so tender to Betsy while her empty soul healed. "Thank You for being a Wonderful Counselor. Continue to guide Sharon and bless the alters in Jesus' name."

I am quiet again and then I saw in my spirit a lot of fighting going on in a house. This is the house I grew up in as a child. My mother is yelling, "I never wanted you to be born; I never wanted you!" She went on to tell me, "You were never born, you were captured!" I never understood why she would say such painful things to me.

It is amazing how I survived my grandfather and my mother with all their rage and hatred. I never experienced love coming from my mother. She never had an encouraging word either. My mother always told me, "Sharon, you can't do anything right."

I asked Jesus, "Why did you bring me back here?" Jesus replied, "I wanted to show you how hurt and hollow your mother was. Your mother had nowhere to go with her pain and went in and out of mental institutions. Sharon, you had Me in your life when you were thirteen."

Jesus showed Sharon her mother's shattered heart. Jesus continued, "Your mother had several abortions, and gave up another baby for adoption. Sharon, I spared you from these experiences and gave you two beautiful daughters."

Jesus continued, "Your mother couldn't love you because she couldn't love herself. She was so needy that she couldn't handle your needs. Your step-dad really loved you. But his love and care couldn't reach or help your mother.

I am crying. As a child I wanted to suffocate myself. I see an image of my heart held together with masking tape.

Jesus focused my thoughts on how damaged my mother became. My struggle with food is like my mother's struggle with alcohol. It is only by God's grace that I could love and care for my mother in our home when she came down with cancer. I remember telling someone that Jesus brought her to my home to be healed, but then I heard Jesus say to me, "No, I brought her to your home to heal you, too."

The cancer gradually took over my mother's body. My mother was changing.

She was grateful that she was not alone and that my kids were there. The week before my mother died she started having memories about her past. My mother accepted the Lord before she died! One day she put her hands on my face and told me she loved me. Several days later both my husband and I were sitting on her bed, my mother died in my arms with a tear going down her cheek.

While caring for my mother the Lord was increasing my compassion and understanding for her.

Roger pointed out, "Your mother trusted Jesus as her Savior, and she told you she loved you. Did you forgive her?" I told Roger, "Thirty-five years ago I surrendered my mother and stopped blaming her. I was aware she had a very troubled and difficult life."

I never missed my mother after she died - we never had a loving mother-daughter relationship, so there was nothing to miss. I do miss my step-dad. I had lots of fun with him, and have happy memories of our time together.

He married my mother when I was about four. I lived with my grandparents until I was six. I think my grandfather is my real father. The Lord told me that in this Scripture, when I was struggling with my relationship with God the Father, **John 1:12 Yet to all who received him, to those who believed in his name, he gave the right to become children of God--children born not of natural descent, nor of human decision, or a husband's will, but born of God.** Every time I read this Scripture the Holy Spirit contrasted "human decision with husband's will." For me the focus was on the word human decision, and not being married as in husband's will.

Roger noted the trauma my mother went through since her early years. I said I was aware she had several abortions from a diary she left out one day. I know I represented something very painful to her. My grandfather controlled her. She had a kind of love for him, but in the end, didn't even go to his funeral.

2/14/17 Jesus shows me Hearts on Valentine's Day

I see my heart with masking
tape to hold the pieces together.

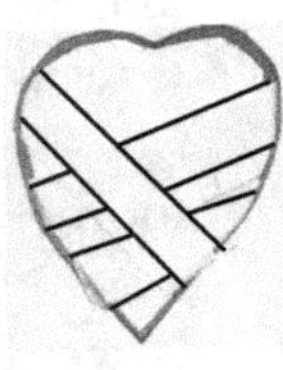

My mother's heart shattered, and
unrecognizable as a heart.

My grandfather's heart is
black and smashed.

Jesus' heart is real
big and royal red

Roger sympathized, "This is hard on you." I replied, "This is showing me truth." Roger commented, "When Jesus shows us things, there is healing." I had cried on and off throughout the two hour session.

Roger prayed for receiving more insight.

The Lord is taking me back to a conference I attended years ago, called "Healing the Heart." We are all in a circle and I clearly heard my grandfather's words, "I am sorry." Tears ran down my face. I only remembered him as fearful and abusive.

The scene changes again and now I am sitting on a rock with Jesus. My grandfather is sitting across from me on another rock. I asked him, "Why did you abuse me when I was a little girl?" Addressing me as Sherry, my grandfather replied, "I was very sick." I told him I am 70 years old and still working through the pain of what was done to me. He looked devastated, I see tears coming down my grandfather's face and Jesus gave him a tissue.

Jesus shows me an image of my grandfather's heart. It is smashed, looking black. Sherry is telling Jesus how hard it was being there with her grandfather. I don't ever want him to touch me. I asked Jesus, "What do you do when someone tries to destroy you?" I asked my grandfather what he did to destroy my mother. My grandfather replied, "Evil people do evil things. I loved your mother, but I was sick."

Jesus is showing me four different hearts. My grandfather's heart is smashed and black. My mother's heart is very fragmented in pieces, and you can't even tell it was a heart. My heart is fragmented but held together by masking tape. Jesus' heart is very big and bright red.

I asked Jesus why he brought me here. He said He wanted me to see my grandfather's pain and repentance. I see my mother now sitting on a rock with my grandfather; their hearts are healed and restored. Jesus said, "Some people repent and get a do-over in this life. Restoration is possible on the earth, and sometimes healing comes late in life. Tears are running down my face.

My grandfather and mother disappeared. Just Jesus and I are on the rock. I am sitting on Jesus' lap. He spoke, "The Father created you in your mother's womb. I am sorry it was such a difficult journey. I always loved you." Then Jesus quoted **Philippians 4:19 And my God will meet all your needs according to the riches of his glory in Christ Jesus.** Jesus is saying that my needs would not depend on the family I was born into.

I responded, "I desperately needed You, Jesus. My mother and grandfather found You late in life."

Roger responded, "Jesus was there all along to love you on the difficult journey." Tearfully I tell Roger, "It has been a tough road." Roger replied, "I can't even comprehend how difficult it has been for you." Roger asked, "How did you feel when you saw your grandfather's pain?" I replied, "I still felt a lot of terror, and I can't imagine what happened to him to make him do such things."

Chapter Nine

CHERRIE

Session with Roger 3/1/17

My past week was intense, but beneficial, with some positive emotions developing. I have moved from feeling frozen for years to defrosting. With the tearful experience at the altar, and forgiving my grandmother, I had dealt with the fact that my grandmother wasn't safe either. The lie I believed all those years was that my grandmother protected me.

A pastor at a healing conference talked about choice, that there are always two trees, not just in the Garden of Eden but everywhere in life. The two trees represent two choices which allows freedom to choose—one good, one bad.

I am seeing two trees and a table of food. I don't know why I am often so destructive with food choices. If God has something good for me, why am I choosing what is bad?

My brother sent me an e-mail on Wednesday with a picture of my grandfather's house and the graveyard next door. He thought of sending this picture because he was working in a town nearby. He remembered staying overnight there when he was very small. He remembered going into the basement and seeing a coal chute. I wondered why someone would take him down into the basement at a young age. Had he experienced abuse there, too?

DEVASTATION

I was watching a **WAR** take place. I was either viewing or actually close by. There were two tanks fighting. **ONE BIG TANK** went up to the **LITTLE TANK** and put the **LONG FIRING GUN** inside the little tank and **BLASTED**. The blast **DEVASTATED** the little tank and all **FOUR MEN** were **SHATTERED** in mid-air.

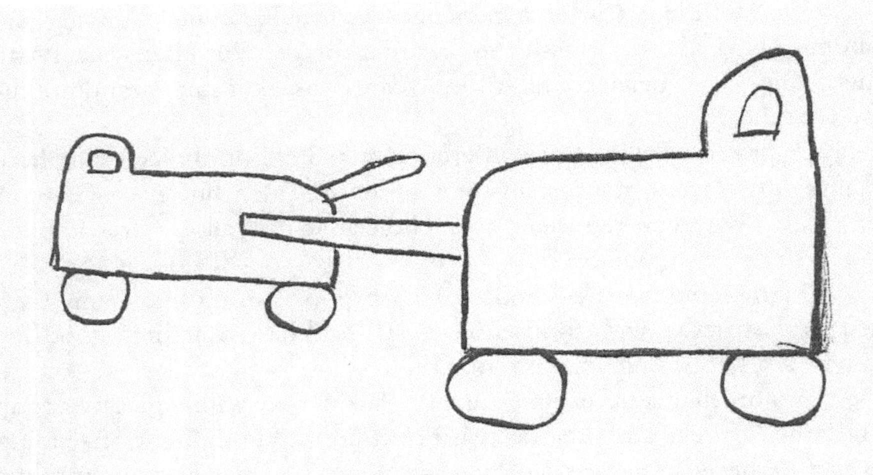

I was praying with Roger when the Holy Spirit changed my thoughts, and I visualized my grandfather putting a cane around my neck and walking me down the stairs like a dog. His handyman Ken is now coming up the basement steps with his dog. My uncle is there too, coming up the back porch dressed like a dog! I am on the floor like a dog. I am now sitting on the edge of the kitchen table taking liquid from a spoon. I can't hold up my head.

I exclaim, "Jesus, where are you!" But Jesus is there the entire time to show me horrific memories that needed to be revealed and healed.

The scene changes. I see someone dressed in white, holding a cane. I am inside somewhere. The person claims, "I'm Jesus, and you are bad." I know this is not Jesus, because Jesus is standing right next to me. This fake Jesus then gives me a choice. I am aware of an axe, but I can't see what is happening. The fake Jesus says, "Because you are so bad, we need to have a sacrifice." They put a tiny baby in my arms and said, "It's either you or the baby!"

Cherrie, my alter, is five and the real Jesus says to her, "I was the Sacrifice, and I'm sorry evil touched your life. Whatever they make you do, I can heal it."

The bad people take the baby from Cherrie's arms and lay her on the altar. "It's you or her!" they shout. Cherrie would not do it. So they take the baby off the altar and put Cherrie on the altar. "We warned you; it is you or her! You will get one more chance."

The Holy Spirit reminded me of the baby rose I chopped off with an axe at the therapist's office many years ago. I knew that my acting out with the axe and the baby rose bud, was what Cherrie was forced to do to the baby.

- Now I know I'm bad
- Worse than a dog
- Scum of the earth

Fake Jesus continues, "All evil belongs to Satan. You belong to Satan now; he possesses your body and your mind." They make Cherrie drink the baby's blood and eat the baby's flesh to remember what she had done.

I see them smearing the baby's blood all over Cherrie's naked body. They keep putting Cherrie's head up and down in a bucket of water or a toilet. Someone says, "You are baptized in the name of the father, son, and holy ghost." Someone says, "We finally broke her will."

****

The true Jesus takes Cherrie to the cottage. Jesus lets her rinse off in the shower and then has her take a bubble bath. All the abusers are left behind. Then she dresses and goes into the living room. Jesus is there holding the baby, who is not dead anymore! The baby is healed and happy, and a little bigger than what she remembered.

Jesus declares, "I am the Sacrifice." He shares with Cherrie a book about His story, how He died on a Cross.
Jesus said,

- I chose you
- I love you
- You are not bad; they are bad
- They made you do bad things
- There is nothing they can do to you that I can't heal
- If you let me in, I can live in your heart and mind
- You can have the mind of Christ that passes all understanding
- The evil things they made you do will fall by the wayside

Cherrie says, "I do want you in my heart and mind." Jesus then baptizes her in the tub in the name of the Father, Son and Holy Spirit. Jesus gives her a dry dress to put on.

Jesus says there is one more thing I have to do, Jesus gives Cherrie Communion. Jesus declares:

- When you eat this bread, you will remember Me
- When you drink this cup, you will remember Me
- When you remember what they did, you will not remember the pain of it

"Did Cherrie really experience this?" Roger responded, "What they did was wrong, and Jesus made it right. And Jesus even took care of the baby."

I realized it did happen when Jesus undid it all! That transformation was more real to me than the shadowy memories of what they forced me to do. Roger said, "The blessing and the love Jesus has for you takes command over the evil and destructive things they did to you."

Roger said, "They were programming you to believe the lie that you deserved their abuse." Then Jesus came along, and He shone the light of truth on the lie. The truth, no, you are not bad. It goes back to **John 8:32 Then you will know the truth, and the truth will set you free.** They programmed you with a lie, but Jesus cast out their untruth.

I had believed what they said about me. Roger responded, "At that point you were buying into it because of the horrific nature of the trauma." I said, "The trauma did take over my mind."

I saw Jesus and all the things he was showing me. Jesus had made all things clean and new. The evil part was foggy. What Jesus was showing me was clear.

I have been struggling my whole life with what they made my alters do while not understanding why I felt so bad, so guilty. What they did was always in my mind even though I could not remember it. When my two year old daughter became sick, I actually believed it was my fault that she got cancer. My abusers probably told me my children would suffer because of me.

I asked, "Should we now try to integrate Cherrie?" Roger said a prayer for integration. Then he talked with Cherrie and asked, "Now that you had that experience with Jesus, and you know and trust in God's unfailing love, and Sharon is okay, would you want to be integrate with Sharon? Jesus gave Cherrie a puzzle piece where the split occurred many years ago. Cherrie's puzzle piece is the last one at the very bottom of the heart where it comes to a point! Sharon told Cherrie she loves her and thanked her for the pain she endured. Sharon will be so much stronger now that all are INTEGRATED.

Session with Roger on 3/15/17

I told Roger I was emotionally drained after seeing the movie, "Shack." I slept for three hours after I got home. There were five things that caused deep emotion in me, during my session with Roger. They were:

- being surrounded by alcoholism in childhood from age five years old.

- being an unwilling victim of Satanic abuse and then seeing the dead baby alive and well in Jesus' arms
- seeing and hearing my grandfather say he was sorry for the abuse
- forgiving all those involved in the horrific abuse I endured as a child
- blaming myself for my daughter's cancer

Roger talked about my progress, that I am no longer numb without emotions. There were other positives in the past two weeks. Between my shoulder surgery six months ago and my following therapy, I was beginning to feel more stable, more complete, more peaceful, and more energetic. Roger affirmed, "Sounds like these are good things." My emotions and energy were coming back, and I was sharing with my family more of my past.

I asked Roger, "When do I move beyond the abuse?" Roger said, "Based on past experience, once integration is complete, you are still going to have memories of these things, but you are not going to be hindered by them anymore."

Roger prayed, and I started to get an image of two people in a tug-of-war. I immediately asked Jesus to come into this picture and help me.

Jesus tells me I was in a struggle with Satan. I could see two people on the opposite ends of this very large saw, pulling back and forth. I realize I was on one end, with Jesus by my side, and Satan is on the other end. Satan tells me, "You are bad, and I'm not done with you yet."

Satan is now gone, and Jesus and I are sitting on a rock talking. I feel God is equipping me, putting a covering over me, and I hear these words, "I am in your heart, I am in your mind, and I want to strengthen you." Jesus has given me the mind of Christ, yet I am still struggling with my physical body. No matter how hard I work at it, I don't seem to lose weight.

It's as if I've carried the weight of the world in my body since I was a little kid. People accept and live in the bodies given them, and I don't. I feel it is a burden having a body. I ask Jesus, "What am I supposed to do with the struggle I have with my body?"

Jesus answers, "Surrender it. You are still believing a lie. You are still holding on to it." Satan is claiming, "I still have your body." I tell Jesus, I'll surrender my body. I am going to surrender the burden I feel having a body. I will also surrender all the sadness I felt as a kid and not wanting to live in a body." I also tell the Lord, "My hands feel painful for what the alters were forced to do."

Jesus responds by saying, "You will carry truth to hurting people!"

- I made you strong
- I want you to change your focus
- I want to give you a new set of lenses for you to spiritually see
- I want you to be a light to a hurting world
- My light shines through a cracked vessel
- You have to let Me change what is on the inside in order to fix your concern about your outside
- I love you with an everlasting love, including your spirit, mind, and body
- You have one body and one spirit which are not separate
- All parts of you need to be working together
- The alters of your shattered heart had to surrender too, and it is no different for you in your struggle with food

The prayer time closed with thoughts about the clothing the Lord put on me today.

Isaiah 61:10 For he has clothed me with garments of salvation and arrayed me in a robe of his righteousness.

Roger talked about many SRA survivors who have issues about their bodies. Roger said, "They could have programmed you not to want a body."

Roger suggested I get a Surrender Box just like Jesus had for my alters. Roger told me to put a slit into the top of the box and tape the box so I cannot take back what I put into it. He suggested that every time I have an issue with my body to write it down, surrender it to the Lord, and put it in the box.

A TENDER SHOOT

6/4/02

While several of us were praying together the Lord used the Isaiah 53:2 passage to give me an image of a "YELLOW FLOWER" peeking up through the earth. I could see the flower looking like a small child with TWO EYES PEEPING OUT. I thought of the part/parts that lived inside of me. If God could surface the tender shoots in the spring, He surely could also surface what seemed frozen to me.

Isaiah 53:2

He grew up before him like a **TENDER SHOOT,** and a **ROOT** out of **DRY GROUND.**

Chapter Ten

May (Mae)

Session with Roger March 29, 2017

I brought my Surrender Box in to share with Roger, my surrendering of all the things that have a hold on my body.

Roger opened up in prayer to free up any remaining alters. I prayed about my continual struggle with my body. "If there is anything that was done to me in secret, I pray that you would expose it." **Hebrew 4:13 Nothing in all creation is hidden from God's sight.**

I was getting an image of something I drew years ago. Beth Moore had talked about how a tiny crocus is able to push its way up through the frozen ground. If the Lord could push up a delicate crocus through the frozen earth, He surely could push up anything I needed to be exposed and healed.

A scene unfolds: I see a little girl, and it's Sherry. Sherry is standing next to Jesus, looking at this tiny crocus I drew with two little eyes peeking out from the ground. I had colored it yellow. Sherry asks Jesus, "Are you trying to birth something here?" I see now a head and then a body coming out of the ground. She is now all the way out, and this new alter is sitting in a patch of crocus. Sherry says, "Hi, who are you?" She replies, "I am five and have been buried for a long time." I ask Jesus who she was, and Jesus says, "She will talk." Sherry speaks, "I am Sherry and I am Sharon's inner child."

Sherry tells the little alter that she watched, "Long Lost Family" on TV which is about people who have never known their birth mothers and are searching for them. Sherry is telling her, "I am really happy you are here. I am sorry you have been buried.   I saw your eyes years ago, but I guess you were not ready to come out." Jesus and Sherry are sitting on a rock and wondering what the alter's name is. I don't know why Sherry is there instead of Sharon interacting with an alter.

Jesus says, "The alter has a yellow covering because I have been protecting her." Sherry asks Jesus, "Can we give her a name?" Sherry asks the little girl, "Do you know why you came out today?"

The "Long Lost Family" last night was about a 24 year old woman trying to find her birth mom. Her adoptive parents had never told her that she was adopted. At age 24 she learned this unsettling, disturbing truth.

It was even more painful when she met her biological mom, who revealed why she was given away at birth. Her stepfather had raped her, getting her pregnant. Deborah's biological mom never told anyone.

Sherry feels the alter was carrying this very secret. Sherry begins calling her Little One: and says, "Little One, I am sorry you had to hold the secret in all these years by yourself. I know how it is to feel all alone."   Sherry hears the alter speak these words, "You are your grandfather's daughter!"

So the shame I saw in this biological mother is the shame I saw in my mother's behavior all those years.

Sherry asks the Little One, "Can I come hold you? I love you Little One." Sherry tells her that she has a Father God in Heaven, and He is a perfect Father, and that He loves her. Sherry says the woman on the TV is special and so are you. Sherry tells her, "I am happy that you are here. I am happy that God created you, and you should not carry this shame." The alter declares, "I represent the reason why your mother hated you."

Sherry wants to know if Jesus brought the Surrender Box. Sherry is trying to write the word "shame" on a big piece of paper. Sherry asks the Little One, "Do you know who Jesus is?" She replies, "Yes, I knew He was going to come get me." Sherry tells her, "It was not your fault how you were conceived, God is your Creator."

I am feeling more sympathy for my mom. I am replaying the movie in my head, especially when the biological mother met her daughter for the first time.

Sherry keeps asking the Little One, "Can you give me your name?" Little One replies, "Why don't you call me Secret?" Sherry replies, "No, that name sounds like you may be carrying guilt and pain, so let's give you a different name." The alter is struggling to come up with another name, so Sherry says, "Why don't we call you May (Mae)?" That was my mother's middle name, and that is the season when crocus come up. Little One likes that name. Then Sherry asks May if she wants to put her shame into the Surrender Box. Sherry rolls up a little scroll with the word shame written on it, and May puts it into the Surrender Box. May wants to know what will replace this shame when it has taken so much of her life. Jesus says, "You can't fill your life by yourself, but you can do it through me." May says to Jesus, "I need you to live in my heart because I can't do this alone, I don't know how to live."

Now May, Sherry and Jesus are playing ring-around-the rosie. The two little girls are picking flowers from the crocus patch.

I now see the three of them behind my grandparent's house, at the bottom of the hill, by the brook. The girls are putting the crocus flowers in the water, and Jesus begins baptizing May. She is still asking Jesus, "How do I live? I only know how to live shame that is all I know." Jesus says, "One day at a time. As I grow in you, you will live a truer life." May says she feels much freer after the baptism. May confesses, "The only thing I was carrying was the family secret."

Roger asked me how I felt about the whole scenario. I felt like how Deborah did when she was 24, and found out how she was conceived. Roger reminded me I had a sense that my grandfather was my father all along. When I talked about my grandfather, I sometimes said "father," not grandfather. It also didn't make sense if Lola, my sister, and I both had the same biological father why didn't my mother say the painful things about her birth as well?

Deborah's mother didn't tell anybody; it was her secret. When her mother told her why she was given up at birth and who her dad turned out to be, the news was extremely disturbing and painful.

The mother and daughter were going to start a new relationship, but my mother carried that secret to the grave. My mother passed away with her secret, and somehow I carried her shame. Roger quoted, **2 Corinthians 5:17 Therefore, if anyone is in Christ, the new creation has come: the old has gone, the new is here.**

That picture I drew years ago was empowering. God pushing the alter up. Roger declared, "The new birth in Jesus cancels out the first birth!"

There was peace in knowing for sure the truth. I realized my Mother's life-long pain when I saw the mother on the TV program and all that she had endured.

Roger asked, "As far as May is concerned, do you feel that chapter is done now? Or, do you think May has some other things to deal with?" Sharon responded, "May was carrying a secret and I have been carrying the shame in my body."

Roger asked, "Is there more May needs to deal with or is she ready to integrate? The secret is out; the shame is in the Surrender Box; and she is safe now." Jesus had baptized her.

Roger opened in prayer again, "Lord, we don't want to get ahead of You. Is there more that May needs to surrender? If it is your will for May to integrate now, may it be done. Give Sharon and Sherry wisdom in talking to May. In Jesus name, Amen."

We are back to the brook; the little girls are picking up crocus floating in the water. The secret has been overwhelming for May to share. The girls go to a violet patch behind the garage and are picking flowers, too.

They go up to the sandbox. The two little girls are sitting on one side, and Jesus is across from them. Sherry wants to pray. May wants to know what the word "pray" means. Sherry explains, "I am going to have a conversation with Jesus and Father God: this is prayer." Sherry closes her eyes and said, "Jesus, help May; she had a tough day; help her uncover anything else she needs to remember. Help her to dump it in the Surrender Box. Help her to let go."

Jesus, Sherry, and May are all sitting around the sandbox. May is saying, "My grandfather said to me, 'I am you father, I am your creator, you are mine.'" Sherry replies, "That is a lie!" Jesus speaks, "I am your creator; I knit you together in your mother's womb; you are mine; and your name is written in the Lamb's Book of Life." Jesus speaks, "Your earthly father has no power, I have the power and the victory." Sherry says, "Did he say anything else?" May responds, "He said, 'Your body belongs to me.' I was his to sacrifice." Jesus is telling May that He is the only Sacrifice and that He died as a Sacrifice to set everyone free. That those who believe in Him are free. Jesus told May, "I am sorry when you were a little girl your grandfather had so much power over you. I am sorry for the lies he told you. I baptized you so your body is free. The only thing your grandfather said that was true was that he is your biological father. Everything else is a lie."

May is taking the sand from the sandbox and putting it in the dump truck, saying, "I don't belong to you, I belong to Jesus." She puts the sand in the dump truck as a surrender. She takes another shovel of sand and says, "Jesus is the Sacrifice, you weren't. You don't own my body, Jesus paid the price. Jesus died for me." She is riding the truck around the sand box.   She then picks it up, and takes it over to the Surrender Box, and dumps the sand into the Surrender Box for all the lies she believed.   May says, "This is very overwhelming."   Sherry asks May if Bop did anything else to her, or did he say other things.

May is asking Jesus, "How do I handle knowing my grandfather is my father and my mother hated me?"

Jesus talks about how difficult the circumstances were with His birth and what Mary had to carry alone.   Jesus is also telling her it is not about what you did, but what I have done to set you free from your trauma.   "There is not one thing I can't undo.   Don't look back, look forward!"

Sharon asked, "Can we integrate May?"

Jesus takes them to a happy place, Mountain Pool.   May, Sherry, and Jesus are sitting in the shallow end of the pool.   Sherry asks May, "Are you tired of living alone?   You can integrate, and come and live in me."   May wants to know if she can bring the crocus with her.   Jesus gives her a piece of the puzzle; tells her to go find out where it belonged in Sharon's heart.   Her piece fits right next to Cherrie, near the bottom of the heart.   When they INTEGRATE, a whole bunch of people are having a party inside of Sharon!

Roger said, "Sharon, this whole thing is coming to fruition, coming together."   Sharon replies, "It is so amazing how I was watching the Long Lost Family, because I don't watch much TV.   This episode had been the first time that a daughter was raped by her step-father giving up the child at birth." Roger said, "Somehow I think you are going to sleep better tonight."   Sharon shared, "I had been feeling lately so overwhelmed, and that is exactly what May was feeling."   Roger said, "Now, you have seen healing."

12/2019

It is my birthday today and I am still trying to come to grips that my grandfather was my father.   I am grateful to finally know the truth of my birth, which made me understand my mother's hatred.   Yet in spite of Roger telling me:

- You are a new creation in Christ Jesus, behold all things have passed away, all things are new
- The new birth cancels out the first birth

There still remained this sick feeling inside about how I was conceived.   Then one day I was alone with the Father, reading a prayer book by Silvia Gunter, and it talked about how the Father's DNA overrides the biological father's DNA and instantly I felt complete peace. It was just the Father God and I alone. I was created by My Father in Heaven.

Chapter 11

Coming to the End

Session with Roger 4/11/17

I had gone over the notes I had taken over the last six months. I was able to connect them to my drawings from years ago. I marveled at this, like WOW, Lord!

After my alters surfaced so much of what I had gone through, I could better understand my hatred for my body. It was painful confirmation that my grandfather was my biological father.

Roger opened with prayer, "Thank you Lord for all you revealed and healed." I prayed, "If there are places where I am still stuck, help me Lord--I just give that to you."

As I quiet myself, the scene before me unfolds, and the Lord is walking me to a pool. We are at a diving board. Now I am sitting on the diving board, and I am really afraid. I ask the Lord, "Why am I so afraid? Why is this so difficult for me?" I am retreating from the diving board, telling Jesus I want to see Him go first. Jesus is on the diving board and jumps into the water. I now could jump off the diving board into the water knowing that Jesus would be there to catch me. What resonates is that there was never anybody there to catch me when I was growing up! That is the basis of my anxiety. I was crying as I asked Jesus, "What to do with this deep hurt?"

Jesus said, "You had a lot of hurt and pain in your life, and I always got you through, protected you in ways you could not see."

I knew my Dad was a good dad, but he was unable to do anything with my mother. I now see myself sitting on my Step-Dad's lap, and he is reading to me. He is telling me he loved me. I knew that he loved me.

I needed to surrender all the dead ends, including counselors who could not help me. The constant rejection and their lack of understanding of my shattered heart made me believe the lie that there was something really wrong and unfixable with me.

Roger said, "There is a list of things you need to surrender to the Lord. These are things that, as you look back, you had not released before. "

Session with Roger 4/25/17

Roger began, "Lord we thank you again for another day of life. Thank you for the blessings. You know every detail and have love and concern for Sharon. You know what is going on with the alters, so we put them in your hands. You are the Wonderful Counselor. We ask that you show Sharon whatever she needs to see. We want your will to be done, so bless, guide and give wisdom. In Jesus' name, amen."

I am thinking about Puppet having a heart put inside him and nothing else yet. "Lord, you healed Puppet, and I need my heart healed. Whatever was severed I need reconnected again."

Then it was like I took my heart out of my body and gave it to Him. The Lord was putting a new heart in me. I can see veins and muscles, and I also see Him in the middle of my heart.

Roger continued in prayer, "Now Lord Jesus, is there anything Sharon needs to see or deal with today in addition to what you have already shown her?"

I visualized Jesus is with a shovel, digging a hole, and then a box appears, and it is a Surrender Box that is really pretty much like the one I have. Jesus is putting the old heart in it and burying it because it was now dead. I feel like He is putting some flowers on top of the ground. I tell Roger, "I don't feel sad about burying the heart because it didn't work the right way. It only kept me alive. It was like my shoulder it needed to be replaced or fixed."

This was actually a second heart that I remember Jesus giving me. I got the first heart about fifteen or twenty years ago. I was very involved with a recovery ministry and I had to leave to allow the Lord to do spiritual surgery on my heart.

My second new heart is not like Puppet's heart, free floating in his body. Jesus was in it, truth was in it, but it was not fully connected. In healing the alters God is also healing me. I see His power work in me as I see it work in them.

Connie, my scribe, said she saw the new heart glowing throughout my whole body, and I was being healed physically, mentally, and spiritually.

Roger observed, "One of the things you said was, I will heal you as I did the alters. You saw my power with the alters, and I will heal you. Are all the alters integrated?" I said, "The ones that came out are all integrated."

Roger asked, "Are you aware of any other alters inside?" I said, "No." Roger replied, "I am wondering if there are still more alters inside? Just the way it was said made me wonder." I said, "Please say it again," Roger said, "I will heal you the way I did the alters." When I drew my heart I felt something might be missing. There might be room for one more puzzle piece.

Roger said, "But now you have a new heart." I said, "With a new center." Roger follows with, "But is the heart complete now? It is going to be interesting to see. Close your eyes again. Lord, we do thank you for all you have done today. We thank you for showing us your power and authority. Lord, we thank you for the new heart, and all that Sharon has experienced in our time together. Are there still more alters inside or is the new heart whole now?" Sharon said, "I hear the word whole."

Roger concluded, "Lord, we do thank you again for another day. You never forget to amaze us--the help, the blessings, the healing that takes place. Lord, you said you were going to heal the brokenhearted. We have been watching that healing take place, and we give you praise and glory for that. In the days to come I pray if there is anything else that Sharon needs to work on You will help her with that, You are the Wonderful Counselor. Make Sharon completely healed emotionally and every other way. Lord, we give you praise and honor, and we thank you for being so active in our lives, for being so caring and so loving. In Jesus name. Amen"

Chapter Twelve

Mary – Last Alter Surfaces Over Two Years After Last Session with Roger on 3/29/17

Session with Roger 9/10/19

I told Roger that I am aware I am anxious due, in part, to what appears to be a new alter. Both my husband Dave and my friend Dot detected that I am not myself. Dave didn't even want to leave to go shelling at the beach because of the space I was in.

I begin praying and visualizing. I ask Jesus to give my new alter a name. Jesus replies, "Call her Mary after my earthly mother, because she suffered much for my sake."

Roger asks if I said anything yet to Mary about integration, and observes, "I think many alters have shared their stories—Mary might not have much to contribute to your understanding."

I tell Roger I still have difficulty connecting with positive emotions. I don't feel fully alive. No ember, spark, no fire. I do get some connection with praise music, watching others who show that spark and joy.

Roger says, "Let's go back into the Conference Room where Mary and Jesus are together." I tell Roger, "I still have issues with food." Roger responds, "First, we will find peace and integration for the alter Mary."

Mary has tears and shares her problems with eating. Roger prays for wisdom for Mary: "Heal her broken heart which will bless both Mary and Sharon."

I offer my prayer to the Lord, "I lift up Mary to you. Father, thank you for her tears and the connection we have on food issues."

I am in the Conference Room. I see Mary is on the little rocking chair, and Jesus is on the big one. Roger asks the Lord, "Can Mary now share with Sharon a need for integration?" Mary is reaching for Jesus' hand and saying, "He's my friend." I feel like Mary is trying to comfort me instead of me comforting her.

I ask, "Mary, why did you look so dirty and black?" Mary responds, "I was there from the beginning, as Jesus was there before time began, and I was part of your heart before they abused and destroyed you. It is from all the things the other alters went through protecting you." Sharon asks, "Mary, do you still feel destroyed?" Mary responds, "My hope is in Jesus." "Mary, do you know why I have no emotions?" Mary answers, "They will come; they are just around the bend."

"Mary, how do we give up the pain of food addiction—it seems I have had that forever." Mary replies, "Jesus will give us new life and replace our food addictions with good things, He is the Bread of Life."

"Mary, why didn't you reveal yourself two years ago, when the other alters did? Mary replied, "Because I am your gift, and you are now ready for me."

. Mary had already accepted Jesus into her heart, after watching the other alters.

"Mary, any pain you need to tell me about that I haven't been told?" "No, my heart has bubbles in it and is alive and well. I have been delivered."

Sharon asks Mary, if she knows what integration means? Mary responds, "Yes, I won't be alone anymore. Jesus will complete what He started, and I know I will complete your heart. I am your last puzzle piece."

Roger asks, "Mary, are you ready to INTEGRATE?" Mary says, "Yes, Jesus lives in Sharon, and I will join the other alters."

Roger asks Jesus, "How do you want it to happen?" Jesus, Mary and Sharon are holding hands around Sharon's heart. Jesus says, "Ready, set, go," and they all walk into Sharon's heart.

Roger ends with, "Now we find out what is next to come."

My Completed Heart

2/14/17 Betsy integrated into my heart.

- Jesus was showing Betsy her part of Sharon's heart with a puzzle peace that fitted into the heart's bottom left hand corner. (page 116)

3/1/17 Cherrie integrated into my heart.

- Jesus gave Cherrie a puzzle piece where the split occurred many years ago. Cherrie's puzzle piece is the last one at the very bottom of the heart where it comes to a point. (page 125)

3/29/17 May (Mae) integrated into my heart.

- Jesus gives her a piece of the puzzle; tells her to go find out where it belonged in Sharon's heart. (page 133)

9/10/19 Mary integrated into my heart.

- My heart has bubbles in it. Jesus will complete what He started, and I know I will complete your heart. I am your last puzzle piece. (page 140)

11/4/17
Dr. Shannon Culpepper
Freedom & Fullness Seminar
"Deliverance Seminar"

Jesus pushed
darkness upward

Jesus pushed
darkness up to my
heart

Darkness pushed out of
my heart by Jesus. It lands
like a bowling ball on the
floor

One hand over the
other pulling up the
"divider"

It feels like my
organs were
moving around

I could see the Hand of God
pull out the "split" that was
dividing me

2/18/18
Patricia King's
Glory School
"The Person of the
Holy Spirit"
Lesson Three

Chapter 13

Restructuring

I first saw the image of "The Split Child" during my month long stay at a Christian Clinic in 1988. More images came during a 2017 "Freedom & Fullness Seminar" taught by Dr. Shannon Culpepper. I visualized Jesus inside of me pushing up the darkness until it gathered in my heart; Jesus then pushing the darkness out of my heart until it dropped on the floor like a heavy bowling ball.

About three months later I was doing a study by Patricia King called "Glory School." We were studying Lesson Three titled "The Person of the Holy Spirit." I saw an image of the divider that separated "The Split Child," being pulled up and out by God. The darkness was already on the ground like a bowling ball.

I marveled at the details the Lord communicated to me. I was in awe how the Lord was showing me the darkness and the split had been conquered!!

I was at my daughter Jen's home during the Christmas week with my husband. I could not sleep and got up around 3:30 a.m., turned on the Christmas lights, sat down and listened to a sermon by Sarah Jakes Roberts called "Restructuring." This YouTube video had a powerful message for me, and I knew it would be the title of the final page of my testament. Messages to me from that video:

- Restructuring requires you to let go of something – something must die

- You can't say "greater is He who is in you" and count yourself as an "underdog"
- Belief broke the curse. Surrender it and let go!
- You need to restructure the belief system; You need to bury the disbelief
- Addiction must go

The Lord had healed all of my alters. They have worked through their traumatic stories and surrendered their pain which were my stories and pain. The alters had been baptized by Jesus, and then integrated back to the part of my heart where they broke off many years ago.

Years ago, I was able to lose fifty pounds as I surrendered different parts of my past. Now I am left with about twenty pounds that I need to mentally and physically surrender. It is not so much the weight but being liberated from the power it has over my mind.

I am sold out to Jesus, but it hit me when Sarah Jakes Roberts started talking about an "underdog." I knew the Lord was talking to me through her. My alters had moved past the dog programming I experienced as a child. What the Lord did for my alters He will continue to do for my present body issues.

I became a compulsive overeater to push down the trauma. Now that the pain has been healed, I need to trust the Lord for what He will lead me to do with my body and my life.

Lord, I surrender all that would hold me back and down. Break the curse that seeks a stranglehold on my body and my belief. Lord, you are all I need. Love, Sharon

9 781716 521799